Jorge A. Livraga

# THE ELEMENTAL SPIRITS OF NATURE

Translated from the Spanish by Julian Scott

Jorge A. Livraga

# THE ELEMENTAL SPIRITS OF NATURE

NEW ACROPOLIS
CULTURAL ASSOCIATION

ISBN 84-85982-67-3
D.L.: M-12980-1999
Published by: New Acropolis, Spain

First published 1985
English translation published Julian Scott
Printed and bound in Espain. March 1999

Illustrations by:
Josef Machynka
Magister of the Vienna Academy of Art

*Dedicated to a friend of my youth*

*called Gemon, who taught me about*

*the Elementals*

*J.A.L.*

# CONTENTS

# PROLOGUE

According to the classical rules - which have lasted for thousands of years precisely because they are effective - the natural structure for any form of communication is made up of three essential parts:

**1) The Prologue**: in which the Author explains why and how he is going to deal with the subject.

**2) The Subject itself or Logos:** what the Author wishes to say to the Reader, in the case of a book.

**3) The Epilogue**:which adds the finishing touches and gives a final justification for the subject matter, being at once the summary and the moral.

This short Manual will adhere to these rules because it aims to be effective, within the limitations of the Subject and the Author.

The 20th century was to be a golden age for those who dreamed of it, but for those of us who have had to live through it, it turned out to be an age of iron; the most appalling wars broke out, the loftiest ethical edifices collapsed and the natural home of man - Nature - was polluted, and so, in consequence, was Man himself. But as the end of this strife-torn century draws near and the age-old monsters of materialism, atheism and evil emerge from the chaos of the collective unconscious, the old law of compensation has brought with it a redeeming interest in the Occult Side of Life.

This interest, which could become the driving-force of extraordinary transformations in society, has also been affected by the environment in which it has developed, and we now find anyone and everyone holding forth about Occult Sciences, forgetting that every Science, whether it is exoteric or esoteric, has its First Principles, its Theory and its Practice. It is dangerous to improvise, and if one wants to invent something, one has to do so according to the natural laws which govern inventions. To ignore this basic methodology leads to a kind of "science-fiction" where the non-existent is mistaken for the real and realities are completely overlooked, the end result being a hotch-potch of ignorance and uncertainty which turns the attention towards the instinctive and ephemeral, producing a lot of smoke and very little fire, and so quickly burning out what could have become a beacon of hope and a centre of knowledge, as an alternative to the intellectualism which turned the 20th century into a failure and a torture chamber for millions of human beings.

In the face of this apogee of farce disguised as Truth, we wish to hold up a small but truthful Light. And this gift is not offered in a spirit of self-interest, in the expectation of approval or any other kind of reward; it is a pure and simple act of Love.

To be perfectly honest, we had never planned to write on this subject and to lay it before the public view. But on seeing so many humbugs churning out their fantasies, and watching as those sublime roses are turned into the blood-drenched thorns of devil-worship, when their scent should be an incentive for sensitive souls to go in quest of them and to find them, even in the darkness, we decided to lift a tiny corner of the age-old veil. A veil which was not necessary when Men lived in contact with the Subtle Worlds and their inhabitants. When they did not fear them. When they did not try to use them as instruments in the service of their passions.

This short Manual is, then, a step towards hope, towards the belief in a new and better world. The central theme, the Elementals or Spirits of Nature, will be dealt with in the simplest possible way, setting out from a view of the cosmos which will enable the reader who is spiritually prepared, to discover a world of beings which are not supernatural, but exist in their own dimension, whether or not they are perceived by those who are trapped in their own sphere centred around the bodily senses.

The materialism of the 19th century could not conceive of television or the sound of the human voice being transmitted over a distance, riding on waves of energy for which the thickest walls or physical obstacles are as nothing. Nor could it imagine the possibility of viewing the bones of a living being through its flesh. We have no wish, however, to overwhelm the reader with well known examples, but simply to remind him or her that the "Supernatural" is only supernatural for those who have a narrow concept of what is "natural". Ultra-violet and infra-red rays exist, even though the naked eye cannot perceive them as images and forms. The Elementals exist, even though the vast majority of men have lost the ability to perceive them. Those beings which modern esoterism calls "Elementals", which Hinduism calls "devas" and Christianity calls "angels", are as varied and as different from one another as, say, are cypresses and clovers, even though both of these belong to the vegetable world.

Let us make an effort together. Let us become children again, let us once more believe and understand. Within the great failure of the 20th century, let us create a survival module which will set out for a bright and true horizon, leaving behind the fears of the night and the corporized breath of the Great Beast of ignorance, sterile intellectualism and despair.

# CHAPTER I

## THE MEGACOSMOS

According to the ancients, there are cycles in the Universe of such length that for humans a single one of them would merit the name of Eternity. However, this is really no more than a figure of speech, since man cannot conceive of Eternity, only Constant Duration. And even this Duration cannot be fully imagined, since we do not understand when it begins or when it ends, though that does not make it unreal.

Any attempt to rationalize this phenomenon escapes us, as water runs through the prongs of a fork. All we can perceive is the trace of moisture which the liquid has left behind on the utensil. But it is the only thing we can get and so we cling to it in order to catch at least a glimpse of that which is beyond the reach of our consciousness.

What we call the Megacosmos - to give it as suitable a name as we can - constitutes the totality of galaxies with all the millions of light years which separate them from one another, materially speaking, and everything else which, because of its non-material nature, is

*What we call the Megacosmos constitutes the totality of galaxies*

unreal for man's senses, but evident for his mind. It is... Mystery. On this matter, true esoterists never speak; and if they find themselves obliged to do so, they allude to it in such a way that no definitions can be drawn from what they say, for these, by their very nature, limit and therefore negate the very thing to which they refer.

At the beginning and the end of the Megacosmos are the Enigmas, all that we do not and cannot know while we are still subject to our human condition. Nor can we even define it by negation, since to negate something is in itself to give it some condition and to open it to discussion.

Our only inner certainty is that in it is God; but not the "good" God, or God with any other humanized attribute. Simply God. Simply Mystery. It is that which we do not know, made sacred by its super-human, para-rational dimension which is totally outside the scope of our conceptions...The Hindus called it the "Non-Thing", as have all the esoterists of all nations. Everything is there and nothing is there. And we do not exclude ourselves, that is, Human Beings.

## THE COSMOS

From the first Duality - Theos and Chaos, Purusha and Prakriti or whatever name one wants to give it - was born the Intelligible Cosmos, the one which is possible for us to understand. From the eternal entropy of the Megacosmos we now pass to another entropy, the Cosmos, which is dynamic, in constant movement and transformation, and in the great Game of Maya, reflects itself in thousands of mirrors. In it we are born and die and are reborn myriads of times.

The Cosmos is guided by a purpose and has a pyramidal structure which promotes the selection of the fittest with the intention that they may help the less fit. In this World there is truth and falsehood, pleasure and pain, life and death. The cycles are defined and defining; there is Karma. Merit is won and lost. The number of elements which compose it is fixed and always the same, but their combinations are so numerous that we could well call them "infinite".

Here everything is valid, everything has its own properties, but at the same time everything is relative. We know the large by comparison with the small, which in the presence of something even smaller becomes comparatively large. We have an idea of movement because of the relation between two or more bodies; on whichever we fix our attention, we call that motionless. If, for example, we are travelling in a motor car and we concentrate on a mountain by the side of the road, it will seem to us that it is our vehicle which is moving, but we only have to lower our eyes and fix them on the glove-pocket of the car for the mountain to appear to be moving away from us.

Our blessing and our curse in this Cosmos is that always, at some time, we attain what we desire and prove to ourselves what we believe to be true, and vice versa. We perceive God if we believe in Him; faith is the heart of all intelligence.

This Cosmos, which is intelligible to us without the need for explanations, is our home: the Galaxy to which we belong, the Solar System to which we belong, the Planet to which we belong, the Country which we inhabit and the ground on which we tread.

Our excessive consubstantiation with our material body and with its environment has crippled the ability of our senses, with the exception of the primary sensations, to perceive any life which may be developing on a vibratory frequency which exists outside, whether above or below, our narrow sevenfold spectrum, of which we have developed only 4 rays, and are fixed at this 4th one, perceiving the other 6 as extended extremities of a Hexagrammaton surrounding a central point.

# THE MICROCOSMOS

In a broad sense, this is constituted by Man, and in a strict sense by every man or woman. At this stage of evolution the scheme of human life presents itself as a basic duality: Me and my Environment. I am the central point of this scheme and my other 6 possibilities of consciousness are reduced, when considering the Golden Egg of my Environment, to 5 which are my 5 senses. The Pentagrammaton is born. Behold Man!

The tools of 20th century Man, however sophisticated they may be, are no more than extensions of our arms or our feet. Radio is an extension of our ears. Television of our eyes. An artificial satellite is no more than the transmutation of the stone which a child throws up into the air. They are all extensions of our possibilities, but do not increase the depth of our perceptions.

The culture of the 20th century is a "horizontal culture", which expands rapidly like a mass of oil, but as it expands, becomes thinner and dilutes into a thin perimetral line, producing gaps and tears in the centre. Its over-extension creates mirror-images and its characteristics force it into confusing kaleidoscopic games of artistic, social, economic, psychological and religious surrealism. There are no roots and no future prospects. The system is blocked.

Man can move his body at high speeds, but he travels as if trapped in himself, blind and deaf, with no capacity for philosophical wonder and even less for metaphysical projection. There is no conception of goodness, only welfare; no appreciation of peace in the heart, only the comfort of one's backside; no deep reflection, only speculation. The World has become transformed into a basketful of captive crickets which make a lot of noise but cannot transcend the confusion of a desperate prattling, as they lie about stunned by their own psychological collisions.

The option is cruelly simple; to die a madman or to hold one's peace and try to live fully in all the directions of Space and Time.

A good opening is to find out about other dimensions, where other types of beings dwell. Those which, when Man was not contaminated by his own external and internal traffic jams, he was able to perceive.

For this it is essential for Man to feel once more that he is a part of the Universe; neither its master nor its slave, simply part of that Macrobios which is the Cosmos, in which the Microcosmos or Anthropos has his place. Let us leave aside the contradictions invented in the Hall of Mirrors and go towards the harmonizations which are natural to us.

CHAPTER II

# THE UNIVERSE AS A LIVING BEING

This is not a working hypothesis or a theory; it is a reality. The One-Life IS and is in everything. What is commonly called life and death is mere transfiguration, changes in appearance according to the angle from which they are observed.

The entropy which we mentioned earlier is a quality of the universe by virtue of which nothing is lost, nothing is gained, and everything is transformed; and bodies are mere shadows cast by their spirits onto the dimension in which these spirits have their consciousness

Thus, when man thirsts for a body, he is physically reborn, since his accumulated karma rides on his desires and his fears. One is always where one desires or fears to be.

This is possible because, although matter seems to be discontinuous, an immense range of energies binds everything together. Energy is continuous and its continuity is not affected by changes of direction and differences in intensity. The sea, stormy or calm, at low or high Even Existence is only the first quality of Being.

*Entropy is a quality of the universe by virtue of which nothing is lost, nothing is gained, and everything is transformed*

Since Being IS, by its very definition, it also Exists. That is to say, it lives. The life of Being or God (of this God that we can perceive and whose Works we can interpret since he is God-In-The-Cosmos, or The Cosmic God, or Anima Mundi) is the Jiva of the Hindus, the Mahaprana which is the supporting base of all the pranic modules, however small they may be, which are modelled by Intelligence and sustained by Will.

The mineral, the vegetable, the animal, the human, the heroic, the world of the gods and the Column of Light which unites them - all this lives, breathes, vibrates or moves, or grows still.

Anyone who has succeeded in opening his eyes to Life, can perceive it all around him. An intelligent life, determined to BE. It takes on the forms and densities it needs. It becomes fish in the water, fawn in the woods, rock in the mountains, lightning in the sky, kiss on the lips, glint on the sword, murmurs in the silence, fleeting and translucent forms in the nights, voices which speak to us from deep within ourselves, music of stone in the old temples and immaterial architecture in Wagner.

Everything lives for ever within this cycle of Life, within this Macrobios whose Spirit is Our-Lord-God. Death does not exist.

## PLANES OF VIBRATION IN THE UNIVERSE

Even though the Substance is One, this Substance vibrates and emits a huge variety of differing shades which give rise to manifold opportunities for the appearance of life-forms. In our Universe, and more specifically in our Solar System, there are 10 planes of vibration accessible to the understanding of Man. Of the highest 3 we shall not speak. The remaining 7, which are directly relevant to Man, are, from "above" to "below", as follows:

*In our Universe there are 10 planes of vibration accessible to the understanding of Man.*

**SPIRITUAL WILL:**

Called "Atma" by the Hindus. It is the highest and most sublime and is, as it were, contained within the 3rd Cosmic Plane of the Solar Triad or Logos. Of this Plane of Spiritual Will, no detailed description can be given since it lies far beyond the grasp of human understanding. It is beyond the mind and even the intuition. It is the Great Amenti of the Egyptians; the uppermost angle of the Rhombus of the Magicians, of the Magical Square bathed in the Light of Amon, and it is the Great Blueness, the Heavenly Nile whereon sails the Bark of Millions of Years (a way of referring to the Boat-Which-Sails-In-Eternity).

**INTUITION:**

Called "Buddhi" by the Hindus. The Plane of Light which is the source of all Spiritual Enlightenment, represented by the halo which encircles the heads of the images of Christ or of Buddha. It is the World of the Devas or Angels and of those who have attained Great Holiness. On this plane, the relation of Subject-Object-Quality is simultaneous, since Time - at least from the human point of view - does not exist there. It is the Mansion of Love, of Concord. There is Shan-Gri-La, the Marvellous Garden where the lotuses never close their petals according to the old Bud belief of the Chinese and Tibetans.

**THE MIND:**

Called "Manas" by the Hindus. This is the realm of the series of numbers and the archetypes. Here on this plane is the root of Man's Mental Spark, the so-called Causal Body, the luminous shadow of his still undeveloped potential on the two higher planes. It is the Dwelling-place of the totally differentiated Self or Ego. It is the Plane of the Ideals, of the Pure Ideas, of the Individual Being. For the Egyptians it is Horus-On-The-Horizon. It is the plane of the vehicle of the Holy Spirit and the Substance of the higher part of the Cup or Grail.

## THE MIND WITH DESIRES:

Called "Kama-Manas" by the Hindus. It is the Hall of Mirrors. The seat of multiplicity and of the multiplication of forms. It is the Treasure Chest, the Jewel Box of glamour or reflected light and of darkness; Pandora's Mansion. Hope and Fear. It is the Forge of Vulcan where the Artefacts are hammered into shape. Where ideas run after one another, find one another, are joined and separated. The "Mayavirupas" or idea-forms are born and developed here, before they fall downwards or rise upwards. The desires live on this plane and anguish makes its appearance.

## THE PSYCHE OR SHINING DOUBLES:

This is the vibratory world in which the Archetypes and desires take on organic forms constituted by subtle matter or polarized energy. Many of these forms have their counterparts in the most solid world, the physical; and although they are called doubles, the real doubles are the organic robots which are their shadows. That is why the Egyptians used to call human bodies on this plane Kha or "Shining Doubles" and recognized their power over matter. The Hindus call the bodies which are made of this psychological matter "Linga Sharira", bodies which cannot be laid hold of by physical means. The energy which is polarized onto archetypes and which gives them their substance, it is what the Medieval Cabbalists knew by the term "Astral Light", on its coarser level, for there is another "Astral Light" which is not on this plane but on the 2nd, which is where the Sambhogas of the Saints and Buddhas develop.

Each of these Worlds contains in itself the reflection of all the rest, as well as its own. Thus, although the Records of Memory, which in India are called the "Akashic Records", do not have their root here, since they need "mental substance" to be recorded, it is on the mental sub-plane of this Psychic plane or World that memories are reflected and cause the past lives of men to reach their present consciousness and become visible to them. Without the Astral Light, they are like film which has been exposed but needs light to be seen clearly. With it, many people are able to receive visual impressions of these memories with relative ease. In this World also there are the reflections of things to come, for as it is closer to the Causal Plane, the impulses pass through this region before they reach the physical Earth.

Sounds, colours and some perfumes, have their origin in this World. We shall see further on how the Elementals take from this plane the basic substance of the harmonious elements which with they adorn the world of Nature.

**ENERGY:**

Known as the Pranic Plane by the Hindus, the plane of the Key of Life, for the Egyptians, in its most earthly expression, which took the form of *the Ankh*. Here energy is constantly being polarized in a highly complex way by means of a thermo-electric dynamics (to use modern terms which bear some resemblance to what we really mean), and the ratios of relative speed, distance, and cooperation between the vectors of force are regulated to maintain a mean density of matter. The effects of these forces are what form the physical bodies, as iron filings are given form by the force-field of a magnet. On this plane the densest bodies of the Elementals exist and it is here that they produce their ordinary phenomena.

**MATTER:**

Where the Hindus situate the "Stula Sharira" or human physical body which, with its physical environment, is what forms the normal "habitat" of men, the field of all their actions. It is the World of Substance, the Malkuth of the Cabbalists, always moved and coloured by the Sekinah. It is, in effect, the world of duality par excellence. If the classical definition of Matter is anything which can occupy a place in space, let us make the qualification that that space must be physical. As physical as Matter, and that space is no more than the Shadow of Energy, the limitation of Freedom - insofar as we give that controversial word the meaning of an attribute of Being, beyond the restrictive materialistic image of beings as a dialectical plurality lacking the sufficient Reality to Be in themselves.

Decelerated Energy becomes Matter visible to physical eyes. Trapped and crowded together in gravitational nodules, energy is transformed into a "thing", with its properties, some of them intrinsic and others which it receives from more subtle planes, as in the common case of radioactivity, a recorded expression of the innermost workings of Matter. But what we call "innermost" refers also to "depth" and entails an escape from the narrow prison of matter, a prison which is really only made of bars, for the winds of energy are continually passing through it. And let us remember that the very bars themselves are no more than arrested or decelerated wind.

For esoterists, there are two Worlds which have no reality: the first one that we mentioned, because it is so far above our range of perception or understanding and to which we only referred because it is inhabited by the quality of Will, the philosophical synonym of Existence; and the last or Physical World, because it is only the passing Shadow of Divine Objects, in movement towards Objectives which are not perceptible from the materialistic point of view. But in this unreality we have our body of flesh, of which we humans have become so fond, and for no other reason than this we have to give it importance and validity, since things have the value that we give them. Leaving aside the Real Value which each thing may have, this is the way Man sees it. All-important and circumstantial. When one is thirsty in the desert, a glass of water is worth more than a ton of diamonds or a Pompeian painting. Life is held to be good and death bad. Everything is governed by this primordial duality. The One-Life is not commonly perceived.

## CHAPTER III

# WHAT ARE THE ELEMENTS?

Traditions which stretch back over thousands of years tell us that the Cosmos is constituted on the basis of a single Element. It is the concept of a unity prior to the dualities of the intelligible world and their subsequent harmonization. But if the Archetype is one, then the substance must also necessarily be one in essence. This is what Democritus was referring to in his writings when he spoke of the "atom" as the indivisible "part" which supported the cosmos. It is not the so-called "atom" which Man has been disintegrating for the last half a century that the ancient Greeks were referring to. What we nowadays call an "atom" (which literally means without parts and is therefore indivisible) is no more than a micro-molecule which is itself made up of many different elements. The atom of the classical thinkers is beyond anything that is known by modern science.

But on the manifested plane where we move and act and which we are able to perceive and understand, we can affirm that there are four Elements: Earth, Water, Air and Fire. These four form two interpenetrating generative crosses, since Earth and Air have a

*The four Elements also correspond to the four lower planes of Nature. In Alchemy they are the four strata which are formed inside the Athanor.*

horizontal movement, whilst that of Water and Fire is vertical. Thus Earth is made fertile by Water and Air is made fertile by Fire. These two crosses give rise to vital elements which are characterized by their force and their beneficial effect for man: material fertility and energetic fertility.

These four Elements are not to be understood as physical Earth, physical Water, physical Fire and physical Air, but as much larger groups, which are represented on an exoteric level by these four physical elements. They also correspond to the four lower planes of Nature: Earth to the Physical, Water to the Energetic, Air to the Psychic and Fire to the Mental. In Alchemy they are the four strata which are formed inside the Athanor. At the bottom Salt; in the middle, the two forms of Mercury, and in the upper part, the Sulphur crowned by the Phoenix of Fire, a form of the fifth Element which in its natural state is impossible to find since, due to the fact that it is still in its formative stage, it is very unstable.

The four Elements influence the qualities of things,so we may hear people talking of plants of Water, stones of Air or of zodiacal signs of Fire, though not always with a knowledge of why they are so described. In fact, the four Elements are like four fundamental forces or musical notes in our system of Nature, within its overall tone of Dynamic Unity which enables these four Modes to interpenetrate one another and to be built into the architecture of the Divine Plan which rules us.

## WHAT ARE THE ELEMENTALS?

They are forms of life within the Elements. It is obviously very difficult to explain the basic characteristics by which they can be defined, since their bodies are not on the strictly physical plane where our visual and auditory senses function, or, to put it in a better way,

*The Elementals are forms of life within the Elements.*

as their bodies are not in the right "position" for us to see them, although they may be in some way on the physical plane; and so we tend to think of them as the empty imaginings of primitive men or the idle fancies of children.

The bodies of these life-forms exist on the Pranic Plane and not below it. However, as the Planes are not neatly divided by any razor-sharp definition, but are linked in an almost infinite series of steps, and as the circumstances of Nature are not always the same (with variations which we know like day and night, the seasons of the year, height, depth, greater or lesser static charge, different atmospheric pressures and different temperatures, rapidly changing states in the atmosphere such as concentrations of Water, Ozone, etc., and apart from all these terrestrial influences those of the heavenly bodies, especially the Sun and the Moon), on certain occasions the Elementals can descend to a level of materialization which makes them more easily visible. But even in such favourable conditions they are not normally perceived.

Let us give an example: a stiff sheet of paper held twenty-five metres away from where we are standing, in full daylight, would be perfectly visible if one of its sides were presented at an angle perpendicular to our own angle of vision. But if it were held in profile and perfectly still, or was moving at the same rhythm as whatever formed its background, it would in practice be invisible for anyone who was not looking for it. Someone who denied the existence of that sheet of paper "a priori" and made no effort to look for it, would be unlikely to see it. This would explain - although we shall look into this question more deeply later on - why the pages of ancient books, clay tablets, papyri and parchments, are full of references to the Spirits of Nature and why on the other hand the cultural elements of our materialistic and "positivist" form of civilization contain no such references.

For a human group which is capable of denying that plants and animals which we see, touch and devour have souls; for those who see nothing more in the loving fidelity of a pet animal, or the vivifying presence and company of a tree or a rose-bush, than forms and colours which they attribute to chance or to more or less invented

*According to esoteric teachings, the Elementals have been present on the Earth for longer than Man himself. When this was no more than a mass of radioactive gases and incandescent matter, the Elementals of FIRE watched over it.*

genetic laws, devoid of any metaphysical attribute, it is difficult to explain the existence and presence of the Spirits of Nature. So although this work is not aimed at the few, and is not "elitist" in intent, being freely offered to all, the writer is fully aware that until the materialistic attitudes inherited from our immediate past have been very substantially changed, many readers will deprive themselves of its benefits by no choice other than their own.

## HOW FAR BACK DO RECORDS OF THE ELEMENTALS GO?

According to esoteric teachings, the Elementals have been present on the Earth for longer than Man himself. Whether as inhabitants, guardians or integral parts of the Elements, they have existed as manifested forms ever since the world has existed. When this was no more than a mass of radioactive gases and incandescent matter, the Elementals of FIRE watched over it; when the stable gases appeared in their chemical composition and in the age of the great winds, the Elementals of Air helped those incipient gases to evolve and to form strata above the recently consolidated earth's crust so as to provide the best possible conditions for the forms of physical life that were being planned. When the gases became heavy and fell as the first waters which then almost covered the entire planet, giving rise to the first truly material forms of life, the Elementals of Water worked on and gradually modified the primitive appearance of the liquid element, at that time highly charged with heavy matter in suspension, which gave it an almost colloidal quality at the deepest levels, while the high waves almost touched the low, compact clouds with their foaming - but not yet white - crests. Later on, like huge slow-moving tortoises, the continental plates emerged, watched over by the Elementals of Earth who gave them conditions of fertility and helped to populate the enormous forests which enabled higher life-forms to develop and made possible the formation of Humanity itself.

Everything in the Universe has a Guardian Spirit. The Planet also had one and it was obeyed by the hierarchies of Spirits of Nature when the days and nights began. It still has its Guardian Spirit and will continue to have it until it disappears. It is the Dhyan-Chohan of the Tibetan Book of Dzyan, the Resplendent Soul which governs the Earth, or the Anima Mundi of the Romans (since it "animates" and moves, and is not to be confused with the Planetary Ego or Spirit of which the physical Earth would be the body).

This knowledge is extremely ancient and we do not know when it originated. All the sources that we have - from the above-mentioned Tibetan book to every other reference from antiquity, mention these processes which, seen from the particular angle of our own scientific viewpoint may sound just like stories to keep us awake at night.

But the Elementals, like the ones whose very smallness and weakness enables them to have contact with humans, also fill the pages of the old books. From Sumer to Egypt and from China to the little that we know of the cultures of America and Black Africa, passing through Polynesia and amongst the inhabitants of the circumpolar regions, and reaching down to the centuries which preceded us in the civilization of Europe, the Spirits of Nature have played an important part in those ways of life which were less contaminated and more natural than our own.

Stories about Genies, Gnomes, Undines, Elves and the whole immense range of Elementals fill the History of Mankind in such a way that without them neither its development nor the telling of it would be the same, as we can confirm in so many instances from the Myth of Enkidu and Gilgamesh to Homer's Odyssey, the Sagas of Arthur and Merlin, or the elementals which taught Isadora Duncan to dance and inspired the glassware of Gallé.

Until very recently, their representations adorned the prows of ships, and they are still portrayed in hundreds of statues throughout the world, whether in parks, or on rocks overlooking the sea.

Grandmothers (... in the times when children were children, adults were adults and old people were old people, whether they held university degrees, noble titles, or were illiterate) used to tell their little grand-children about the Spirits of Nature. Delightful tales whose characters were undines, gnomes, fairies and elves, described with their characteristic forms and life-styles, their prodigies and apparitions.

Even the Catholic belief in a Guardian Angel who looks after little children until they reach the age of seven, has much older roots than Christianity itself, and from Arcadia to America it has always been believed that children, because of their purity and vulnerability, had a Guardian Spirit which saved them from many accidents, protected them from wild beasts and helped them to find their way home when they were lost.

The most curious thing about all this is that in the art forms of such dissimilar peoples, the Spirits of Nature are represented in a similar way. Likewise, in traditions, one hears of the same Elemental beings in 15th century Central Europe as in the heart of India in the 2nd millennium B.C.

If we consider that many of these human groups never knew each other nor had the least suspicion of their mutual existence, the many points of coincidence that we find in their descriptions of Elementals force us to rule out any possibility of chance. It is evident that all of them saw the same or very similar things and that they approached them in the same ways. They attracted them, conjured them, repelled them or feared them... but always in the same way. This can only confirm the fact that all of these different peoples were confronted by a single type of phenomenon and that, by the logic of their common human nature, they treated them a similar way - just as, when confronted by a river, all of them made bridges, some more, others

*Everything in the Universe has a Guardian Spirit.*

less sophisticated, but bridges all the same. And if all of the ancient peoples have spoken of rivers and of the bridges that they built over them, it is evident that the rivers were a real presence. The same is valid for the Elementals, which were for all the ancient peoples a real presence, whose echoes are still audible in our times through folklore and ancient writings.

# CHAPTER IV

## WHAT THE ELEMENTALS ARE LIKE: FORMS AND MANIFESTATIONS.

In keeping with the aim of this short book, we shall now refer to how the Elementals appear to the sight and perception of humans.

We have said in a previous chapter that the bodies of the Spirits of Nature are made of energy and that they are not strictly physical or material in the ordinary sense of the term, although energy is also material and is continually demonstrating its effects on the densest plane of action. What we call "electricity", for example, is energy and is normally invisible; but when it travels along the surface of a metal wire, it is capable of producing material phenomena such as the moving of heavy parts in a machine, which can then move or transfer tons of matter. And we are all familiar with those meteorological phenomena, for example, which take the forms of lightning or "St. Thelmo's Fires".

In the second place, the fact that there are states of vibration which are somewhere between invisible energy and visible matter increases

*They copy the human fashions which are contemporary with the time of their birth.*

the possibility of our seeing Elementals even when we are not making any conscious effort to do so. For although normally the densest part of an Elemental's "body" is on the Energetic Plane, it can, under certain favourable conditions already referred to, be reflected in a more dense and almost corporeal form. This occurs in the etheric zones which are a mixture of "energy" and "matter" and, at the same time, a link between these two planes, the first of which is characterized by a lack of any form perceptible to our senses, while the characteristics of the second are evident to us and can be easily recorded. From this we can infer that Elementals can change shape and move at much higher speeds than we can, since their forms are more unstable and dynamic. It is when these forms slow down that they materialize as corporeal forms, and become more easily visible, whether due to the natural factors that we mentioned earlier, or to the will of the person who wishes to see them. That will must be strong but non-aggressive, since the least instability in it is sensed by the Spirits of Nature and frightens them back into their energetic "retreats" where they will hide behind the optical illusions which come so easily to them and enable them to camouflage themselves in the very Elements they inhabit.

Although, as with all living beings, they come in an almost infinite number of different varieties, a few classic examples of Elementals may be mentioned:

## ELEMENTALS OF EARTH: GNOMES, FAIRIES AND DWARFS:

The word "gnome" derives from the Greek, genomos, which means "one who lives in the earth". There is such a great variety amongst these Spirits of the Elements that they can range from the little dwarfs described in the folklore of all nations, to certain monsters (in the Latin

*Being fond of mischief, they cast psychic spells which prevent adults from finding little things like pencil-cases, spectacles, pins and nails.*

sense of prodigies or alterations of the normal), for which solid rocks offer no greater resistance than a strong gust of wind for us, since the solid earth is the atmosphere in which they move, as we do in the air. These beings are in continual movement, expanding and contracting, and attaining sizes comparable to the largest known mammals. The little dwarfs, on the other hand, are human-like in appearance, and are usually no more than about one foot tall.

These dwarfs or little folk, who are innocent, kind and cruel like children, are the most well-known. They have no ethical awareness and it would be wrong to call them either "good" or "bad".

Mischievous by nature, they like to have fun with people who look for them without knowing how, while they are, on the other hand, the humble servants of true Magicians. Although there must be some of both sexes, neither the stories nor my own observations have recorded any females. In appearance, they tend to look fairly advanced in years, although this does not represent what we call "age", for they live for centuries and do not experience, as we do, the states of childhood, maturity and old age. They appear to be always the same age.

Apart from the head, which is large in relation to the body, as in the case of human dwarfs, they are well-proportioned.

They are always clothed and it seems that, onto a "basic model" of a peasant-type costume, they copy the human fashions which are contemporary with the time of their birth, and keep them for the remaining centuries of their lives. There are no signs of wear in these clothes, although they do not give the impression of being new but creased and crumpled as if they were very old, but indestructible.

Even at the highest levels of materialization, obtained only in special conditions and in places unfrequented by humans, they never emit or perceive any sounds.

They flee from the Sun and love the light of the Moon, of small candles and glow-worms.

*The Monakhos were the emissaries of Hermes who dwelt in hidden places at crossroads and used to look after the hermits of early times.*

Peaceful and calm, they are often still for long periods of time without moving.

There are some, as the children's tales say, no bigger than the size of a fist, no higher than a thumb. These are difficult for adults to perceive, although they themselves must believe quite the opposite, since in the presence or proximity of humans they "hide" behind things, in the darkest corners or, making use of their ability to pass through matter, in the drawers of pieces of furniture which have not been opened for a long time. They enjoy the proximity of children and suggest places and positions to them for their toys, dances and songs, their rounds and games of hide-and-seek. Being fond of mischief, they cast psychic spells which prevent adults from finding little things like pencil-cases, spectacles, pins and nails. When the veil is drawn back, they love to look on as the lost objects are found, sometimes in different places from where they were before, which implies that it is possible for them to move things, although it is much more common for it to be the spells themselves, combined with the bewilderment, anxiety and worry which their tricks produce in humans, that make the people carry the object in their own hands and place it somewhere else without realizing it.

In the times of the Craftsmen's Guilds, before work had become automatized and when people put real interest into it - as craftsmen have started to do once more - the little Gnomes were their invisible Companions in the workshop, their helpers in their tasks. In exceptional cases, some occultists have been able to use their magic to set whole armies of Gnomes, materialized at least in part, to help them in their work; but such kinds of forced labour are very disagreeable to the Elementals, who like to have a certain amount of initiative so that work can be more like a game or recreation.

There is another recorded variety of gnome, though it may just be a mutation of the same type; these ones actually have a normal human appearance and assist travellers on the roads, can speak and give advice, although they do not eat or sleep as humans do, or grow old. Such cases are always found alone and are confused with monks. We

*A certain variety is closely related with humans.*

find the same version in ancient Greece, for the Monakhos were the emissaries of Hermes who dwelt in hidden places at crossroads and used to look after the hermits of early times. It was said of them that they neither ate nor loved, and hardly ever spoke, preferring to communicate by signs. Tradition has it that there was something in their anatomy that made them different from humans: the tips of their ears, which connected them with another type of Elemental, ones which lived in woods and later came to be known as Sylvans. The typical cap of Hermes served to hide this abnormality, which was often related with the Myth of the King with donkey's ears and endowed with parapsychological powers, like Midas.

The Gnomes or little folk can, if they so wish, travel at great speeds and arrive in an instant at wherever they want to be. And in this way they do small services for the Magicians who have a working relationship with them, such as announcing visitors or giving warnings with light raps on pieces of furniture, and others which we shall look at later on. Even though they do not have distinct souls, in a state of differentiation, as humans do, they can seem as if they do under the influence of a practical occultist who is able to communicate with them effectively.

Fairies are also Elementals of Earth, although their many different varieties and the literary and popular traditions have given them such an exalted standing that, in many countries, the denomination is synonymous with enchantress or sorceress, as in the medieval and renaissance Myth of Merlin in the Arthurian Saga, where Morgana appears as a Fairy.

Similar in appearance to humans, their sizes vary between the minutely small and the size of a normal person.

Also ruled by the Moon, they like to gather in places far from any human presence and dance in circles in meadows surrounded by woods. The special form of reproduction which toadstools have, whereby their species expands in the shape of a ring, has linked these plants, in popular tradition, with the "Fairy Rings". And it is true that

*Sirens, as they are known, are elementals of the surface waters of the sea.*

Fairies are most knowledgeable about the occult virtues of plants and minerals. Skilled in enchantments, they inspire natural healers with their strange and at the same time unsophisticated arts, in which intuition is mixed with the garbled memory of a lost science.

A certain variety is closely related with humans, and in the old monarchies they used to bring gifts to the new-born babes, either in the form of blessings, or of curses if there were negative circumstances involved. They are generally fond of children, suggesting games to them and protecting them from dangers, and inspiring them telepathically with actions that will keep them happy and cheerful.

They are attracted by sweets and by sweet things in general, and can be tempted by the smell and the "doubles" of these into the company of humans, whom they would normally prefer to avoid. They like harmonious sounds and circular geometric figures. Their appearance is feminine and I do not know whether there are any males. They are not the feminine counterparts of the Gnomes, as is commonly believed, for their characteristics and natures are different and they "ignore" one another, like animals of different species.

## ELEMENTALS OF WATER:
## SIRENS, NEREIDS, UNDINES AND NYMPHS

Sirens, as they are known, are elementals of the surface waters of the sea. Our word comes from the Latin Siren and the Greek Seiren, meaning "enchanters" or "seducers". Related with music in antiquity, they were said to be the daughters of Melpomene. They are described as having a woman's head and the body of a bird, sometimes a fish. Allied to the elemental forms which rule the sea-breezes, they produce harmonious sounds very similar to the human voice, which they are able to imitate by virtue of their telepathic powers. They could be

*Their masculine counterparts are the Tritons, who were also part of Neptune's retinue.*

placed at the head of the hierarchy of a whole range of Elementals which, though belonging to the Element Water, need a combination with Air in order to live. At the other extreme would be the tiny little creatures which live only in sea-foam, being born with it and dissolving with it, especially on nights of full Moon. According to ancient medicine, these had the ability to bring about extraordinary cures in those who bathed in their waters. They also served Magicians who were able to read omens in the reflection of the lunar light or the "Silver Road" of a full Moon on a calm sea.

There is another variety of Siren which appears on nights when the waves become phosphorescent on being saturated with animal forms, like the so-called "Noctilucae". They bring bad omens and worse memories. They are related to the ancient mystery of the "Sunken Moon" of which we shall not speak.

The Nereids are powerful female Spirits of Nature who served as an escort to Aphrodite, the "Foam-born". They can reach great depths and inhabit underwater grottoes. Their exalted position also made them the companions of Amphitrite, wife of Poseidon, King of the Sea and of Underground Grottoes, the ancient Lord of Earthquakes and of Horsemen, which is why the foaming crests produced by the waves are identified with the "horses of Poseidon". Traditionally linked with royalty and majesty, they were said to protect the difficult manoeuvres of the sailing ships of old when they were carrying kings and emperors. Their masculine counterparts are the Tritons, who were also part of Neptune's retinue; they respond to the Threefold power of the Reflection of the Logos on the Great Mirror or Dark Crystal of Earthly and Fiery origin, which is guarded in Thule for the Crown of the King of the World. Like the Nereids, the upper part of their bodies is similar to that of humans, while the lower part is like an elongated fish, in the manner of a sea serpent. Bedecked with seaweed and corals, pearls and shells, they blow supersonic ethereal sea-shells to announce the passing of conquerors. They know the secret of sunken treasures and on occasions they present themselves as violent executors of the will of their Master, who with his magic

*Like the Nereids, the upper part of their bodies is similar to that of humans, while the lower part is like an elongated fish, in the manner of a sea serpent.*

trident, can keep ships afloat upon the waters, or send them crashing to their doom against the rocks. In past ages they taught human travellers about lost Sciences from submerged Continents.

The Undines owe their name to the Latin, Unda, literally: a wave. They inhabit rivers, especially in those places where they flow between rocks and produce waterfalls and the sounds of foaming water. There are other marine varieties which inhabit coasts and beaches, always in sheltered places, where there are hollows. Above the waist, they have the form of a woman, while from the waist downwards their body has no distinct form, or gives the appearance of being covered with permanently wet linen. With their very long hair, they swim at great speeds and are frequently confused with Nereids. The traditions picture them combing their long hair in very feminine postures and in general they give an impression of weakness and frailty if we compare them with the vigorous and proud strength of the Nereids. In antiquity these creatures were supposed to try to enchant travellers who halted by lonely torrents; they invited them to their grottoes to drink a magical liquid which brought them face to face with their own inner monsters. Only the pure and strong could win through and free themselves from dangerous pacts with the Undines, with their hypnotic eyes and their possession of certain jewels, probably rings, which they offered with the intention of keeping the man who accepted them bound forever within their power.

Nymphs - whose name originally derives from the Latin "lynpha", water, and the Greek "nymphe", in relation with springs and fountains - are Elementals of feminine appearance and extreme beauty, who inhabit lakes and calm waters. They are also guardians of hidden forest-springs. Nymphs are said to be so totally human in appearance that they cannot be distinguished from women. In antiquity they were thought to be guardians of whirlpools and to be both good and evil, displaying at once a capricious and delightful character which could tempt the very Gods themselves.

*With their very long hair, they swim at great speeds and are frequently confused with Nereids.*

From those times we have that most vivid image of the bejewelled Arethusa, reflected in the ceramics of the Hellenistic cultures of Magna Graecia, generally shown on vessels related with water, whether on its own or mixed with wine. Typical is her complicated headdress of pearls and ribbons on her elaborately styled hair. In the Saga of Arthur, which is related with that of the King of the World and Merlin the Magician, it is a Nymph who delivers up from the lakes the magic swords that will bear witness to the royalty of gallant knights. They also appear in the so-called "Germanic Mythology" in connection with Tanhauser. The epitome of Venusian beauty, Nymphs are related with sublimated and jealous love, and in opposition to carnal love. Their vengeance upon men who are unfaithful to them can be terrible. Eternally beautiful and young, they possess that secret of continual youth to which they are condemned, and their punishment is to bestow the controversial gift of not dying. However, their immortality is not the spiritual and conscious kind, but an inhuman one, and tradition has it that through their attempted love affairs they hope to become human and acquire a human sense of life and death. These enigmatic creatures are very knowledgeable about charms, magical metals and precious stones, and in the heart of these they can see things distant, past and future.

## ELEMENTALS OF AIR: SYLPHS AND ELVES.

It is difficult to trace the etymological origin of the Elemental creatures we denominate "Sylphs", although it is probably Gallo-Roman and derived from the sounds produced by the wind on Druidic harps which, like the Aeolian harps of Greece, were usually hung from sacred trees, to be the instruments of some non-human music. These nature-spirits are characterized by living exclusively in the air; they are very difficult to perceive on account of their unstable and fluid

*It is a necessity for them to be constantly moving and changing position.*

nature and their swift, darting movements, so that the researcher has to "pin them down" to something stationary in order to make even the most superficial study of them. This system enrages the Sylphs and causes them pain. Not so much because of the subjection itself, but because they are deprived of movement, without which they weaken and even die. It is a necessity for them to be constantly moving and changing position. Only their head is human in appearance, for the rest of their body, which is difficult to study, is similar to the image we have of angels, though less peaceful and not always with only two wings. Nor are these wings, in the case of this level of Elementals that we are describing, as white, attractive or adorned with feathers as those of the Greek, Roman and Christian images. These have been taken from higher types of Elementals, which we shall refer to later on.

Elves (from the Celtic Faeries) are Elementals of very beautiful and tiny forms. Like ethereal butterflies, they live in the proximity of flowers and in their corollas. Their bodies are anthropomorphic, some masculine, others feminine in form, although this may not bear any strict relation to their mode of reproduction, since they copy human forms. For clothes they wear what look like short tunics of a light material. Their constant movements are similar to those of bees sipping from flowers. Extremely energetic, they have great healing powers, although this kind of work can drain them to the point of death. Their sphere of action extends as far as the perfume of the flower. Flowers without perfume do not have Elves of this type. Certain varieties are very fond of humans, above all of children and of those who have innocence and artistic sensibility. Light excites them and darkness calms them down. They like soft sounds, colours and light reflected in mirrors which are not too highly polished. Their graceful little figures are finished off with small wings similar to those of dragonflies and butterflies, but more beautiful, ethereal and in constant movement, rather like humming-birds. Holding hands they dance in circles and cast good spells. Their sizes vary from a few inches high to less than a centimetre. Sometimes they become still, as if they were sleeping, in peaceful poses. At other times, they

*Elves are Elementals of very beautiful and tiny forms.*

appear to be pensive or listening to what humans cannot hear. They are angelic grace personified.

## ELEMENTALS OF FIRE: SALAMANDERS.

The forms of these Elementals are the least human-like of all. The name by which they are known has a very obscure etymology of oriental origin, which passed into Arabic and links them to the famous university of Salamanca, where the splendour of Islam radiated its fullness into the Later Middle Ages of Europe. Studies in Alchemy were indeed pursued there and under this generic heading is contained a large and varied body of knowledge, including, amongst other things that of the Spirits of Nature, especially those which heat the Athanor, and also crown it.

They can be seen in hearth-fires in the semblance of black serpents, generally in a vertical position, moving swiftly and twisting upon themselves.

The sizes of Salamanders vary, from the small worm-like creatures which move in fires and bonfires, to the enormous ones which produce the curious forms of lightning.

No one who does not have holiness and experience should risk any attempt at contact with these powerful Beings, since they also govern the electrobionic impulses which pass through the human nervous system.

There are metals which send them to sleep and contain them, so that they can lend power to an amulet with forms of Magic too dangerous to be commented upon without the prior commitments that make men incorruptible.

*They can be seen in hearth-fires in the semblance of black serpents, generally in a vertical position*

# OTHER VARIETIES OF ELEMENTALS

Although this topic will be treated in greater depth in another chapter, I think it prudent to point out that the Spirits of Nature which we have described are only the most typical examples of those which appear most vividly reflected in the so-called folklore and traditions of humans.

The range of Elementals is immense, from the Regents of the Planets and even of the stars, to those whose existence keeps the atoms alive.

They were referred to in the Mysteries of antiquity. They were represented by geometric figures, words with no apparent meaning and numerical ciphers which are incomprehensible today. The references are veiled and indirect. It is impossible to classify them all under any one of the Elements alone.

They are the ones who determine the moments of birth and death of all manifested Beings and also of things; of the Souls' crossing of the different thresholds; who move in a space-time which is not the one that we know and inhabit.

They are the ones who watch over the movement of the Clock of History from outside that mechanism of logically related causes and effects; who keep the Annals where the past and future can be read.

They are the Angels and the Demons. Also the Dragons whose breath heats the Earth. The souls of the geological crystals which determine the stratification of minerals and condensed the light of stars which have disappeared from our sight. The Genies of Jewels. Others held captive in the mental forms of the Gods await for aeons the moment when they will direct the delicate operations of the births and deaths of the galaxies: they are the ones who inhabit the comets, whether those which fertilize determined regions of space so that new worlds can be born, or those which are the final remains of other stars from the past drifting towards the cemeteries of stars. There are also the more simple comets which, like valence electrons, bind solar

*The ones who dwell in the interior of volcanoes and clouds; who, with invisible brush-strokes, paint the dawns and the sunsets; who awaken the vegetation in Spring and send it to sleep with the advent of Winter.*

the more simple comets which, like valence electrons, bind solar systems together.

And "closer to home", they are the ones who dwell in the interior of volcanoes and clouds; who, with invisible brush-strokes, paint the dawns and the sunsets; who awaken the vegetation in Spring and send it to sleep with the advent of Winter; who control destiny at the crossroads, in enchanted grottoes and magic mountains.

They are the "Genies" which give and take away gifts. The ones who touch the foreheads of the "chosen" and who cause the feet of those who have fallen into misfortune to slip.

The writer is well aware that in this materialistic 2Oth century of ours these things that have been mentioned sound like science fiction or a tale for children. And this is only natural, for all this knowledge comes from the past and the future. In the present it is unknown and ignored. But nevertheless , it refers to realities, some of which make themselves clearly felt in the lives and inspirations of many people, although the education they receive blocks their capacity for perceiving or imagining the causes, and they accept what happens with stolid resignation, with the characteristic bitterness or the animal-like joy which comes from being subjected to the "dwarfocracy" under which we live. Those who are trapped in the cage of materialism will never be able to perceive these hidden marvels in Nature or see the traces of God's Footsteps on the earth.

# CHAPTER V

## HOW THE ELEMENTALS LIVE: SURVIVAL, SOCIETY AND RELIGION

Although we shall explain this point more fully at a later stage, it must be realised from the start that any observation and study of the Elementals by humans will reflect the characteristics of the former, but will at the same time be strongly coloured and distorted by the characteristics belonging to the latter.

We might think that as modern Man is unaware of the existence of the Elementals, these can live out their lives freely, in accordance with their own natures. This is false. When men were ignorant of the existence of bacteria, and subjected their food to high temperatures by immersing it in boiling water or by direct exposure to a powerful source of heat, they destroyed the micro-organisms and modified them by forcing them to encapsulate themselves, and it mattered little to the phenomenon whether any of the affected parts might be aware of it or not.

In the same way Men, with their different ways of life, all of them more or less mechanized and poisoning, with their own waste products and those produced by their working activities, with their worries and their fears, with their changes of religious forms in relatively short cycles of time for the Elementals, affect them deeply. The Elementals also modify the lives of men, since they play a part in climatic phenomena, in the fauna and in the flora, especially the wild varieties, and even in the individual and collective forms of feeling and thought in Human Beings.

## SURVIVAL AND METHODS OF REPRODUCTION

In referring so generically to the Elementals as we are doing here, it is impossible to lay down any average minimum or maximum life-spans for them, since their variety is so great that some of them - like the ones mentioned earlier which inhabit the sea-foam - appear for a few seconds or even fractions of seconds, while others, like the gigantic inhabitants of the sea depths or the mountain massifs, live for tens of thousands of years. If we go a little deeper into the subject and consider that it is Elementals who govern the variations in the orbits of the sub-atomic elements and of the so-called "Clusters of Galaxies" - since they make up the Elemental Intelligence of every form of energy - we find that the limits just referred to are no more than examples on a "human scale" which can give us some kind of idea without losing us in the unfathomable depths of the infinitely small and the infinitely large, since all questions of size are relative to our own conception of things, and for Man, as Protagoras has said, Man is the measure of all things.

No doubt each time the Elementals are mentioned as the directing forces behind the Powers of Nature - like those which manifest themselves in the constant movement of things, such as electric currents, gravitational attractions or the circulation of the blood - the reader will think that we are corporizing or inventing spirits and beings where there are nothing but relationships between masses of matter or energy.

From the materialistic point of view, that is true, since this particular and restricted vision of the World likes to weigh and measure every aspect and external expression, every property and attribute, without any reference to the "why" of things in its permanent obsession with the "how". Thus, no one can define what "Force" is except by the effects that make it perceptible, although for the exoteric mentality this is enough. And if it is not enough, the slogan "chance" is brought forward and placed at the head of the procession of events. Thanks to the development of technology in the specialty of computer science, we can now make calculations in seconds which would have taken thousands of men their whole lives and much more to work out, and it has been proved that the sum of "chances" by which natural phenomena are supposedly explained is impossible. On the contrary, it is being increasingly demonstrated that there is a "causation" with an evident cascade of causalities which give meaning to Life and to its movements, since computers, which after all are no more than highly developed abacuses programmed according to the intelligent capacity of those who use them, show that even the little that we know is already enough to deny the chance nature of natural phenomena, and that there is a purpose to Life, an immense plan, a dance-like rhythm in the universe. And likewise, that if we consider matter and energy alone as two forms, one less, the other more subtle, of a single thing, the Universe would come to a standstill for in its ecosystem there is a need for intelligent and sensitive elements which can prevent accidents as far as possible, and which like invisible catalysts activate determined processes, and justify a form of "psyche in nature" which we are beginning to discover. That "X" factor, as a number of scientists of advanced conceptions like to call it, we call Elementals

*Red Caps are not as the people of the Scottish countryside describe them.*

or Inhabitants of the elements. This knowledge is as old as Man himself and its remains are preserved in the folklore of all nations, more or less distorted by superstition and fantasy, by customs and necessities; but it is basically true.

Perhaps, to give just one example, the Red Caps are not as the people of the Scottish countryside describe them, always in search of fresh blood to colour their caps and perched on the top of castle ruins; but it is inevitably true that where there have been great battles and slaughters, and where remains of bones and blood-soaked weapons have been left behind, at the scenes of those bloody encounters in which desperation and terror made their mark on so many men and animals, mental and psychic forms linger for a while and somehow impregnate the surroundings, a fact which any sensitive person can perceive even if he or she may not be exactly what is known as a "medium". To discard this possibility "a priori" is somewhat unscientific and even more unphilosophical. Where there has been fire, the warmth of the embers remains for a time, and where water has flowed one will find traces of moisture. Modern techniques based on the perception of infrared rays can reveal, from a patch of coldness completely invisible to our eyes, the spot where a car had been parked on a sunny day a long time ago. But the spirited steeds of technical progress champ at the bit of an almost blind charioteer which is modern Science.

So let us turn to Ancient Science, to Tradition and to Esoteric Knowledge in search of the truth, of which one drop is worth more than an ocean of lies, however well classified and publicized they may be.

Thus, the elementals are born, live and die like all manifested things. The Law is one for all and only God knows why it is so. What is clear for us, though, is that everything which comes into what we call "existence", wears out and changes until its original characteristics are put at risk. The Intelligence which rules us has chosen the method of the renewal of forms in order to preserve what is most internal and important, just as we exchange worn out clothes for new ones when we consider it necessary and have the means to do so. But even this "domestic" example requires a perception of the concept of wear and a calculation of the possibilities of replacement and of the different ways of achieving it, in the light of previous experience and one's present capacity for renewal.

We have to bear in mind our more or less subconscious tendency to see everything in our own human image and to extend the details of our life-cycle to other beings, which is not generally the case, as every life-form has, by the force of its own nature, certain characteristics which are particular to it, notwithstanding the one Law which rules us all. The fact that everything renews itself does not mean that it has to do so in the same way and in the same space of time. Even if those Elementals which are "closer" to men, in other words those which the latter can perceive more easily and vice versa, have a tendency to resemble man, due to the fact that man is an archetype, yet within their evolutionary capsule they differ in many ways.

There are Elementals which are extremely similar to men, and so likewise are the ways in which they are born, live and die. It has even been known, in favourable circumstances, for them to have attained such extreme degrees of materialization by transforming their energy into matter (no miracle: for in the same way the potential energy of a suspended stone is transformed into the cumulus of physical phenomena of its fall; gases become visible and crystallize, passing from the invisible state to the liquid and the solid; or fats and proteins are transformed into visible and tangible adipose tissue in the human body) that they have actually come to live with people, and even had love affairs and battles with them. In some of the cases they have been detected as Spirits of Nature, either on account of their extraordinary longevity, or by it being noticed that the females gave birth without the need for an umbilical cord, or because their blood was a different colour to that of humans.

Likewise they have always been associated with what we now call "parapsychological phenomena" which were carefully observed and recorded by our ancestors, such as noticeably enriching pastures by the simple act of dancing on them, or being able to point with complete certainty to the exact location of hidden treasures, seams of precious metals or underground streams. The old assertion that some Royal Houses had their origin in the cross between a human and a Spirit of Nature, or a demi-god, or even a god, is not so wild as it might seem to us today as we look at the petrified remains of those previously dynamic and creative Royal Houses. But the Law of Cycles is inexorable, and if the ancient kings performed prodigies, the modern ones need the figurative approval of their people.

Other Elementals are as simple as a small energetic tissue, with no defined form or capacity to do anything but float in the vecinity of the corners of houses, or under the roots of trees. The reproduction of these has nothing in common with the human type and we would do better to compare it to cellular parthogenesis. They are simple "shreds of life" which cannot and have no wish to overcome the magnetism of the ground which keeps them floating around just above it. Household cats frequently play with them, hooking onto them with the magnetic projections from the tips of their claws. There are those, too, which are veritable etheric waste products which accumulate in large numbers in places where there are evil smells, miasmas, air heavy with the opaque emanations of diseased bodies, or poisonous perfumes of drugs and malefic plants. They reproduce rapidly, like spores on fungus, and can be dispelled by ventilating with fresh air and cleaning with pure water, letting in direct sunlight and increasing all forms of physical hygiene, from simple soap to clouds of incense and myrrh or storax burnt on a hotplate or on coals. The popular "joss-sticks" are not very effective as they are manufactured commercially with inadequate mixtures of low quality products.

As it would be an unending task to list all the different forms of survival and reproduction among the Elementals, we shall give one example of an average life-form, in a restricted "habitat": the type of gnome which inhabits places covered with pine-trees. These are shy creatures, who because of their great longevity (compared to ours)

*Other Elementals are as simple as a small energetic tissue, with no defined form or capacity to do anything*

wear copies of the clothes which were used by country people in past centuries. They seem to have no reproductive sexuality, although they are prey to extreme sensitivity, so that an emotion with the least trace of violence in it terrifies them and makes them disappear, which they do by subtilizing their forms and camouflaging themselves in the bark and branches of trees.

They feed on the auric excrescences of resins from trees and their perfumes, which is why they usually accept highly scented gifts (by "accept" we mean that they approach them and absorb their emanations).

They do not enjoy the company of men although because of their innate curiosity they are never far away from them and are frequently observing them. They even play jokes on them, which is a childish form of communication, by making noises in the night, playing psychic tricks which make it difficult to find objects just when they are needed, or materialising very fleetingly in the distance so that men and women, preferably young ones, are left feeling confused and fearful. But concentrations of humans terrify them and men's "doubles" crush their own and poison them to the extent of causing them terrible diseases and even death, which for them as for us, means the abandoning of their denser vehicles, with the difference that in the case of the Elementals the individual consciousness disappears as an active entity, merging with the Group Soul of its People or "Ethnic Group".

They have a survival instinct, but death does not drive them to despair as they do not have the imagination to picture themselves in any other situation than the one in which they find themselves at that moment. They find it difficult to remember and have to be almost forced to do so, and although they know many things innately about the properties of plants and the relationships between heavenly bodies and terrestrial phenomena, they only answer if they are asked and if one knows how to question them very patiently, coming back to the subject a thousand times if need be.

As they can never materialize completely, they are unable to speak, although they can hear, even at pitches which are outside our range of hearing. Thus, they communicate with those humans who enjoy their friendship and in some way rule over them, through the medium of signs and general telepathic signals, making communication difficult and at first very slow and discouraging.

In appearance, they always look like little old men, although they themselves can tell the differences in age between them.

At particular times of the year, when it is wet and the Moon can be seen only occasionally through the clouds, around the hour of midnight, they can be seen swarming in the branches of the pine trees. At other times, from the axillas formed by those branches with the trunks or with other larger branches, they extract their offspring who have grown in a kind of ethereal and resin-coloured amniotic sac. Although very small, the newly "born" babes are in shape and proportion identical to their elders, and their development can only be perceived through an increase in size, but there are no other noticeable variations, at least under the special conditions in which, of course, they are observed.

## SOCIETY AND RELIGION. SYSTEMS OF GOVERNMENT.

As we shall never tire of reminding the reader, the great variety of so-called "Spirits of Nature" or Elementals is comparable to that which we might find in the Animal Kingdom; the habits of giraffes and tortoises, of dogs and fishes, are all different from one another. Faced with a problem of such magnitude, we encounter the added difficulty that, as the Elementals are beings whose normal mode of bodily existence is on the plane of energy, and they are therefore non-material and invisible for the immense majority of Humans - and when they are visible it is only in a restricted way - any generalizations are doomed to failure.

Thus, preferring a little truth to a big lie, we shall refer once more to a specific case: the Gnomes which live among the pines.

They live in social groupings, in tribes, forming an extended family, where everyone retains his own individuality, while at the same time being and feeling completely united with the rest of the community. By way of comparison one could think of the relationships which are spontaneously established between human children before they have been contaminated by the education (or rather, anti-education) to which they are subjected by their elders nowadays. For a child, the fact that another one has a different coloured skin, a stammmer or a limp, may be used to make fun of him, but never to segregate him from the group. He will be invited and even forced to stay close to the others and will be taken into account for everything. Where both children and Elementals can express their individuality is only in little secrets and acts of mischief which they do not wish to communicate to others, as if it were to do with something magical.

This society is not communitarian, in the manner proposed by Plato and almost all sociologists in one way or another, perhaps because in the expectations of the Elementals there is no such thing as the notion of progress and they cannot conceive of a "state" in the true sense of the word and according to the Platonic definition.

Each Elemental works and lives for himself but in close companionship with the rest, and apart from a few comical quarrels, knows that he can rely on all of them, although he will be very careful not to interfere with the tasks of others without good reason.

Although their food-supply is apparently assured, at least in the medium term, and their clothes never seem to wear out and they are able to make up their own medicines, they nevertheless seem to be constantly occupied. This should not be understood to mean that they are in feverish activity like bees in a hive, but the spirit is the same, although the rate of work seems to be much calmer and freer. Later on we shall refer to their pastimes and games. Now we shall talk about their work, although in the elementals all forms of activity and ways of living are somehow linked together and it is difficult to know where one ends and the next begins.

The Elementals are very much related with the Plant and Animal Kingdoms, and even with the Human, if we gave them a chance to approach us by living a life closer to Nature. They are tirelessly concerned with such tasks as tending the auras of plants, leaf by leaf, and of meadows, blade by blade. They strengthen the less vigorous parts with energetic "injections", and by a kind of rubbing of fibres against one another they stimulate them and are able to change the orientation of a branch or a leaf, improving the effectiveness of the photo-chemical and physical phenomena which enable the plants to live and help the environment with their exhalations.

They magnetize animals, attract them or frighten them away as the need dictates. They also try to do the same with human beings, especially with very small children, but they are repelled by the discordant noises of machines, by the smell of insecticides and by alcoholic vapours, and most especially by the astral forms of anger and by the idea-forms of evil, usurpation or murder.

The Elementals of the pine forests, except in the rare and exceptional cases when one of them may enter into relations with and render obedience to a human, never move away from a restricted area, normally around a tree for each group and a wood all together.

The form of their society is similar to a Theocracy, since each group has a monarch, but the latter fulfils functions which we could call religious and his mandate does not come from elections or consensuses but from the Grace bestowed by the Spirit, Genius or Totem of the tribe.

The system of government is absolutely natural, that is, "pyramidal" and "popular": an immovable hierarchy, upright and exemplary, which works for and thinks of its subjects more than itself, refusing its attentions to none. The few who are guilty of failing to observe this age-old law of traditional custom are taken prisoner, admonished and put to work under supervision until they gradually become reintegrated into a community which will never remind them of their crimes, if indeed that is the right word to apply to what seem more like simple acts of forgetfulness or products of psychological interference which could only find a parallel on the human level in certain harmless forms of obsessive madness.The king is king as water is water and the Moon is Moon. It would not occur to any Elemental to discuss that or question it. Not having a mind like ours, they cannot conceive of changes or revolutions. They are wholesomely happy with what they know and, in any case, have no aspiration to know anything else. Often, as I have reflected on them, I have been amazed at the timeless wisdom of their systems and how remarkably constructive they are for Nature's Plan, and how many good things they provide without expecting any reward, or even thinking of any kind of payment for what they give to the whole. If they sometimes feel an inclination for some delicacy or for the presence of some human who has "charmed" them, there is not the least possessiveness or passion in their feeling; they simply approach them as the traveller approaches a fire, sometimes more out of curiosity and in search of a soft sweet pleasure than for any other reason.

The Elementals have their secrets, equivalent to our "State Secrets", and I do not know why the king is king or why his assistants are chosen by him from among the many members of the group. I do know that the group as a whole has complete respect for them and that, in own their way, they can give a thousand explanations of the extraordinary greatness of their rulers... But not of where they come from.

They gather in periodical assemblies, on nights of full Moon, where they set up working committees, are kept informed of the progress of the community as a whole, of who has died and who has been born and of any other news, all in a spirit of great peace and experience, like one who performs a rite a million times repeated.

*The religion of the Elementals who inhabit pine-trees is a kind of Naturalism which centres around the worship of the Spirit of the tree which gives them shelter.*

Although they all seem to be equal and I do not know of any schools of thought which make distinctions between them, some are wiser than others on particular subjects and they consult one another mutually. They look after one another. They help one another. In the case of a human who has been accepted by them, they will take him from one to another to try to answer his questions for which one always has to be prepared for very slow and fractional replies which will then have to be fitted together, which the Elementals seem to be totally incapable of doing.

A human who has succeeded in entering into their "enchanted world" and has made friends with one of them, will automatically become his master, since the only kind of relationship they understand is one of command and obedience. Even the sense of companionship which they have among themselves is no more than the sharing of certain prescribed duties and tasks, obligations and rights. Thus, they will obey the human as long as he in turn respects their natures and does not make them do anything which goes against their customs and accepted forms of behaviour. In these cases, they make great efforts to be useful, even to the point of materializing momentarily in order to produce a loud knock on a door or to rap a piece of furniture, in anticipation of their master's return home, for instance. The kind of society they have is so harmonious that when one of them is under the influence of a human - which is exceptional - others will do his unfinished work for him and help him in whatever way they can to carry out his new duties well. Somehow it is a cause of innocent and sweet joy for all of them when someone from the Human Realm, which they very much admire, behaves kindly and respectfully towards one of their number.

Each of them has a name by which he is recognized, although for ritual reasons it is changed periodically.

It can be gathered from their answers that they know a great deal about the natural sciences, including medicine and astrology. But their learning is inherited, practical, and they would be unable to theorize about any of the phenomena that have been registered or which they

*Only one alarm, that I know of, brings them together extraordinarily, and this is the appearance on the surface of the earth of certain enormous Elemental monsters which dwell in the depths.*

see for themselves. They have an innate feel for Art and like to dance and to play rustic astral instruments, as well as to combine the vibrations which we recognize as colours when they have been materialized in bark, leaves and roots.

Later on we shall describe some of the activities of other varieties of Elementals.

The religion of the Elementals who inhabit pine-trees is a kind of Naturalism which centres around the worship of the Spirit of the tree which gives them shelter; they make offerings of dances to it and give it of their astral and energetic energy. The role of high priest is played by the king, but all of them take an active part, for the priest-king is not to be understood as an intermediary but as the master of ceremonies. They have their seasons for these cults, as they have seasons for being born and seasons for dying. Only one alarm, that I know of, brings them together extraordinarily, and this is the appearance on the surface of the earth of certain enormous Elemental monsters which dwell in the depths, and which stretch out a trunk by which they suck them down, apparently feeding on them, in large quantities. I have not heard of any means of defense against the threat, apart from simple evasion and preventive measures.

A tree does not die until its root dies. When that happens, the Elementals who serve it and are its worshippers perform a complex ceremony to transplant the Genius or Spirit of the tree - which outside its material envelope, in the case of pine-trees, assumes a strange tall form, elongated and almost human-like - into a seed or shoot. The whole tribe, assisted by the other Elemental peoples in the wood, if there are any, will collaborate in the hard task of enabling the new tree to grow healthy and free from disease, depredations and fires. When it reaches a certain age and takes on adult form, they will convert it into the Religious Centre of the group and the cycle will begin again.

Apart from this "totemism" which may seem narrow to humans, the Elementals do have a higher religious sense, as if of "Something" which would be the God of the Tree and of the whole Universe, which they see as an immense tree filled with stars, mysteriously coinciding with the traditions of the Tree of Light which are still kept by Christianity, Brahmanism and the Hebrew Cabalists. But they avoid referring to it, thus demonstrating a prudence and a mystical practicality which humans tend to lack.

Thus, individual survival, Society, Religion and the outline of a State, come together into a single way, or rather, sense of living, without much consciousness of immortality, yet not conceiving of death as something final but as one more expression of the cycles of an inexorable and, within the scope of their understanding, immutable Nature.

CHAPTER VI

# RELATIONS BETWEEN ELEMENTALS AND HUMANS

It is true that Humanity, with its uncontrolled population explosion, its alterations, not always for the better, to the "habitat", its tendency towards artificiality and the rejection of everything that does not fit in with the materialistic or exoteric religious doctrines, has put up a "smoke-screen" between itself and its metaphysical environment. But beyond all the ignorance and the cover-ups, things are as they are. Even if a million blind men were to shout in unison that the sun does not exist, it would continue, as always, to give light and heat to all, including those who are unaware of it and deny it. And there is no need to overrate the significance of this: it would do so in response to its own nature and because it cannot deny itself, it cannot cease to exist.

Nowadays, opinion has enormous importance. The pendulum of History has swung from the absolute pre-eminence of the Prophet, of the Divine Leader, whose expressed will became the law for all, to its present antithesis in which number and opinion overrule quality and discernment. The clouded vision of a mentally handicapped person is worth as much (and sometimes more) as the informed judgement of the scholar. It depends on the means of expression available to the one or the other, or on what is most convenient for the vested interests of the day. It is assumed, for example, that a newspaper which prints half a million copies a day, must contain more truth than another which only has a circulation of a few thousand and is presented and distributed less effectively. In this way, humans believe as factual or fictional, truthful or misleading, whatever the hidden masters of public opinion want to make them believe, through the far-readching media of mass communication. The evident fact, frequently demonstrated over the years, that both science and the religions contradict themselves, ought to alert us to the fallibility of certain contentions; but it does not, since the means of diffusion are so far-reaching and have penetrated so deeply into the human subconscious, that the sciences are regarded as true and the religious beliefs as infallible even though in less than a hundred years many of their contentions have been retracted, only to be replaced by others equally hollow and pedantic.

It might be argued that this process reflects the evolving character of a way of thought which searches out the truth and affirms it whenever it finds it; but this would be a fallacy, an unnatural concession.

It is taken for granted, for reasons of evidence, that if a child evolves and becomes a man, the man will retain and reinforce everything from the external form to the Inner Essence of the child, rather than the opposite. It is not the same, however, with the sciences and beliefs, and a few examples, out of thousands, will suffice to motivate the reader to recall and discover other examples for himself.

In the great Universities of Europe, in the middle of the 19th century, it was "scientifically" claimed that machines heavier than air could not fly. In the following 20th century, the great Universities of Europe claim the opposite.

The double censorship of State and Church over all spoken or written expression has been an accepted institution, under the form of the "Holy Office", for centuries, until well into the nineteenth. Today the States and the Churches throw up their hands in horror at the thought of freedom of expression being so restricted, yet behind the back of public opinion they continue to do the same, although to a lesser extent.

The Vatican newspaper L'Osservatore Romano, echoing opinions voiced by Pope John Paul II, has harshly condemned astrologers and horoscopes. But the popes Paul III and Leo X, to mention but two, believed in astrology and even had astrologers to advise them of the best times to convoke the cardinals. By papal order, the ancient Roman University of Sapienza ran a course in Astrology, but this did not prevent other popes, on previous occasions and under the inspiration, one must suppose, of the same Holy spirit, from condemning this science at the Council of Toledo in 447 and at that of Prague in 561. One such theologian, Pico de la Mirandola, stated: "Astrology corrupts philosophy, adulterates medicine, weakens religion, favours idolatry, makes men base, anxious, fatalistic, slavish and unhappy". If we remember that Pope Julius II ordered his astrologers to choose the most appropriate day for his coronation, the contradiction becomes evident. These are not variations of forms or temporary adaptations: they are essential negations and opposite practices. They denote confusion and ignorance, however "dogmatic" their assertions may be.

It is exactly the same with the Elementals. People have believed in them or have denied them as fashion dictated or according to the outlook particular to their own time and place. But beyond all that, the Elementals exist and for countless millenniums Humanity has collected testimonies of their existence; and the most important thing is that these testimonies coincide in different epochs and countries.

The ancient religions which, with their mystery traditions, were far more "ecological" than those of today, had assimilated and added them to their stories of human "saints". Regents of springs and

*The Elementals also made contact with Man and taught him about the healing power of plants.*

mountains, of rivers and roads, the Spirits of Nature maintained physical and psychic relations and dealings with humans.

The reader may have been struck by the fact that since the most ancient epochs man has never managed to domesticate any race of wild animals. It is possible, at most, to tame isolated individuals, but their offspring are born and grow up with the same instincts and danger to Man.

The secret lies in the fact that, through their frequent and intensive dealings with the Elemental World, the ancients were able to influence the Group Soul of a race of animals by the use of enchantments, and so, by combining this with cross-breeding carried out at appropriate intervals, they succeeded in accustoming wild cattle to living with Man, working for him and obediently allowing themsleves to be milked and enclosed. By the same process, wolves gave rise to dogs and panthers and lynxes to cats. Birds, fishes and reptiles were also under human control for thousands of years, although in recent times they have almost totally escaped from that enchantment and have returned to their original wild way of life.

The Elementals also made contact with Man and taught him about the healing power of plants, showing him how to gather them, plant them and transplant them at the right times of year and under the influence of particular heavenly bodies. They taught them to burn resins in order to attract good Spirits and keep away evil ones, to tan hides and ferment liquids. They communicated to them the apparently enigmatic origin of yeasts and, by perfecting them, taught them how not to lose them so that they could reproduce them continually.

They showed them where there were hidden sources of "mineral water" and hot springs; which is why, over the last fifteen centuries, since the Elementals have ceased to receive massive offerings in the temples, the West has only been able to rediscover springs which were last used by the Romans, and by so many other peoples before them.

Even with the help of electronic equipment they have not discovered the lost art of finding a real spring of mineral water.

The Elementals showed men the veins of metals and the stones capable of resisting the tensions of architecture, or those which channel the cosmic and telluric energies under the form of amulets. They also showed them the benefic flowers and their uses for the rites of love and of death. They showed humans the keys to the movements of flocks of birds, shoals of fish and animal herds for the purposes of divination, since the Group Soul of animals can sense in advance the changes of Nature.

The Men of the first intelligent races were instructed in the arts of navigation and sowing by the Elementals, who in turn were responding to the requirements of the Gods. They made Fire descend at particular times from the sky and made it rise up from the bowels of the earth in the sight of men, and they showed them how the thunderbolts inscribed on stones the first signs of a geometric style of writing which was the inspiration for all others.

They transmitted to them the knowledge of the power of natural crystals, that is, of the gems which prudently encircled the wise heads of the first priest-kings. They even instructed them in what the Elementals most feared, because of their magnetic charges: the use of sharpened and pointed forms, made from red and black metals with hilts set first with dew-drops and later with precious and magical stones which are charged with the light of the stars and with the salt deposited by the warrior's hands.

Disguised as "midwives", they taught the first sexed men and women how to have offspring and give birth to them correctly. And they incited men and women to play the games of work, war and love.

They were bridges between the High Gods and humans and they led their protégés to the altars of sacrifice so that the relationship between religion and the mysteries could continue.

Today, appliances have largely replaced the relationship between humans and Elementals. Only in areas which have been left untouched by the present materialistic civilization, are contacts still maintained, albeit precariously.

Knowing that machines, noise, pollution and the vast chaotic agglomerations of people terrify them and destroy them, it is easy to deduce that it is we who have deprived ourselves of the enchantment of that old pact with the Elementals.

But, even if it is to a much lesser degree than in antiquity, the Elementals continue to be in contact with humans.

## SPORADIC CONTACTS WITH ELEMENTALS

European folklore, the most well studied, records contacts between humans and Elementals right up to recent times. Although we shall be explaining something about the nature of the Elementals further on, and not only about the little dwarfs and sylphs, there is one characteristic which is common to practically all the Elementals and which we can mention in advance. Since their bodies are not strictly physical, they possess a great capacity for changing their size and shape, and thus are able to resemble insects or mountains, animals, plants and humans. Certain special conditions make them appear, on rare occasions, in the likenesses of gods and they become vehicles for Them.

Although the popular creed presents them as enemies of all religion, this is a lie and the truth is quite the opposite. What has happened is that the more or less ignorant priests of today's religions which have lost their esoteric content tend to condemn and attack with every weapon available to them the Creatures of Nature, who are naturally passive, but who, when provoked, can eventually react with great

*There exist varieties in areas around the Mediterranean which resist and even enjoy the rays of the Sun.*

violence and produce all kinds of misfortunes; thus are they turned into what they never wanted to be - terrible forces - as a result of the ignorance of those men who throw stones at their own heads and then curse the stone which strikes them.

The Elementals, like almost all beings with etheric bodies, appear more easily in semi-darknesss and in concealed and isolated places, since the discharges of photonic winds hurt their etheric skins, as our physical skin would be stung by a violent sandstorm. But there exist varieties in areas around the Mediterranean, specifically in the highly magnetic islands of the Aegean Sea, which resist and even enjoy the rays of the Sun, and their apparitions are in the early hours of the afternoon, after midday. They are completely human in size and appearance, and in antiquity it was said that their flesh, which can actually become palpable and even solid, was constituted by a concentration of the Light of Apollo, rather like the angelic flesh which Christian theologians have attributed to some angels.

The beauty of these Solar Elementals is proverbial, and those of one sex as much as those of the other like to tempt young humans, who, if they become too involved in their games, suffer nervous disorders which are frequently irreversible, and even madness based on circular ideas and obsessions. Some of the "lucky ones" are said to have lost their power of speech or gone blind.

There is a whole curious fauna of elemental forms which are usually sighted in dark places and whose presence can be sensed instinctively. On other occasions a propitious environment and a human psyche under the pressure of emotions of fear and anxiety make it possible for them to become visible, and even to pass for humans who are asked the way or are given alms.

Apart from magicians and true occultists, those who have the best chances of making contact with them are children, invalids, women in childbirth and elderly people. In the nature of the Elementals, there is a mixture of an inborn desire to help weaker humans, together with a mocking, mischievous and vengeful spirit, the latter especially

*The unquestionably interesting experience of seeing or "sensing" an Elemental .. may be useful to the Soul*

being brought out in the presence of evil or excessively proud or despotic people. Like curious children, they have a special liking for those humans who, having either very beautiful or misshapen bodies, stand out from the rest.

## FAVOURABLE CONDITIONS FOR SEEING AN ELEMENTAL

We are not going to speak about occult matters or about the means by which any Spirit of Nature may be obliged to appear before an exorcist. We shall be referring to the attitude which should be adopted by any human wishing to have the unquestionably interesting experience of seeing or "sensing" an Elemental, with no other intention than the experience itself, in the hope that this may be useful to his Soul.

To this end we shall now indicate several successive steps which will increase the probability of seeing or making contact with an Elemental of the Gnome type.

Phase One: Find a secluded place far from any human habitation, preferably wooded, but which one can reach easily without suffering any anxiety or pain which might disturb the mind. On these adventures, any kind of "mountaineering" or "hiking" should be avoided by those who are not used to it and in whom unwonted physical effort and the consequent emotional disturbances can result in the repelling of real Elementals and the attraction of visions and mental forms which have nothing to do with the Spirits of Nature. It is better not to see anything than to imagine that one sees what are nothing but fantasies.

Phase Two: Analyse yourself in depth, making sure that what you are about to attempt is not for any selfish motives or in order to show off in front of your friends and relations by telling them about your experiences. Consider the possibility that, as a result of your low level of protection or your weak spots, you, the aspirant, may be the victim of unfortunate events: so be prepared, in all sincerity, for whatever God wills. In order to raise the level of safety, do not use any drugs, tobacco or alcohol, eat frugally and lead the purest possible life for two months before embarking on the experiment.

Phase Three: Go to the place alone or with as little company as possible; anyone who accompanies you should, in any case, be looking for the same thing. Camp in a tent or a rustic house, trying to make as little noise as possible and speaking very little. When going to the place where the meeting is anticipated, do not use anything made of metal with the exception of gold or silver, and as far as possible avoid wearing clothes made of synthetic fibres or of untanned leather. Keep you body clean and your mind free from prejudices and fears. Simply wait and see, avoiding all anxiety. Repeat to yourself mentally that you only want to see or make contact with a Spirit of Nature with friendly and peaceful intentions. As long as it is not with any idea of buying but of giving, you can take some sweet-smelling cake, fruits or perfumes and leave them about 50 yards from the place where the observer or observers are to be positioned.

Phase Four: Return to the place of the would-be encounter as often as possible, silently and with the same good cheer. Sit down on the grass or in the branch of a tree and wait, from shortly after sunset until a couple of hours after midnight; do not take anything to drink or to eat except a little water and a handful of dried fruit. Abstain from any other manifestation of a physiological necessity. Stay awake all the time. Set yourself a plan to stay there for a number of days and keep to it, whether you have had good fortune or not. In the case of seeing an Elemental, keep absolutely calm and remember that it is nothing "supernatural", but another of God's creatures, like ourselves. If you want to say something to it and there is a prudent distance between you, do it mentally but moving your lips as if you were actually speaking. As a last resort, try to speak only with the breath in a scarcely audible but firm and confident voice. Accept with good will whatever the Spirit of Nature wishes to show you and never get frightened. If on seeing or thinking that you see something, you yield to panic, run away lighting your path with a torch and never repeat your attempt in this life; rather, from the depths of your Soul, ask the Lords of Destiny to have pity on your weakness, for which you will make amends by doing charitable deeds and making anonymous donations to the needy of the same region where you had your experience. The place of the encounter must be free from all human refuse and the time to be chosen for the experiment should be a period of nights falling between the New Moon and the Full Moon and never the other way around.

Phase Five: To avoid any unforeseen problems, whether or not the observation has been successful, do not tell it to third parties who are unfamiliar with these matters. The best thing is to refrain from talking about one's own experience or to tell it in an impersonal way, after a good number of years have been allowed to pass, since this will decant any false enthusiasms and delusions. Always remember that someone who succeeds in seeing or making contact with an Elemental is no better or worse than one who fails to achieve it, for the paths that the Gods choose for us are mysterious, and it does not bring happiness to try to solve or interpret enigmas which are beyond our comprehension at this stage of our consciousness.

# CHAPTER VII

## RELATIONS BETWEEN ELEMENTALS AND NATURAL PHENOMENA

The rise of the materialistic doctrines which appeared in the 18th and 19th centuries as a more or less justified reaction to the more or less biblical dogmatisms of the Western churches, has converted the majority of civilized Mankind to the creed of chance, discarding the idea that all things have a cause and a purpose, both as individual units and as a whole. The fact of recognising this idea of causality, as was the case for thousands of years, implied the acceptance of a Superior Being or God in which the Universe would be mysteriously immersed, a Being who would not only watch over the evolution of the galaxies, but also of worms and - what the materialists, dialectical or otherwise, least wanted - of men.

The materialistic anathema against the churches and priests was extended to all traditional forms of science, literature and arts. Everything traditional was seen as absurd for, as anyone knows, when an avalanche starts, it does not stop by the wayside, but flattens everything in its path until it has lost its kinetic force. In this way,

*We are taught by the Traditional Sciences that the Spirits of Nature play their part in all natural phenomena.*

taking advantage of the cowards and the "half-hearted" whom even Jesus abhorred, materialistic brutality buried and crushed underfoot the last remains available to the public of all that had previously been known. New things were learnt but the old ones were forgotten, with the result that the vaunted progress of materialistic civilization has remained at zero, bogged down in its own waste, the pollution from which is now endangering the very life of the planet which we call Earth.

It should therefore come as no surprise to us that the colours of sunrises and sunsets are regarded as mere reflections and refractions; the changing tones of the sea as the product of thermo-chemical reactions; and the beginning and end of the life of plants, animals and men as the mere impact of chance. In a world where everything is seen in such terms, nothing can escape from contempt and boredom and this is at the root of the indefinable anguish which is leading even the children of the present form of civilization to drugs and suicide.

We esoteric philosophers do not deny the ceaseless interaction of phenomena, nor have we ever denied it. And I ask in the name of so many venerable predecessors that we should not be confused with the charlatans who have always existed in relation to these subjects, nor with the exoteric priests who were more interested in the perimeter of their full stomachs than in that of their small-minded brains. But one thing is the effects and another the causes, and not just the physical ones which, as we have always known, are at the same time the effects of other previous causes, as the Karma of the Hindus points out, but also those metaphysical causes which give a meaning and a purpose to every form of phenomenalism and phenomenology.

We are taught by the Traditional Sciences that the Spirits of Nature play their part in all natural phenomena. Their Group Souls accumulated the experience which created the growth-rates of nutshells in order to make them more resistant and enable them, at the same time, to keep the necessary moisture in their folds so that the hard packing could break open at the right time for germination.

*The elementals of a higher level added beauty to practicality*

The same experience designed the scales of fish to be flexible and hydrodynamic; it painted owls' eyes on the wings of nocturnal butterflies to scare off their pursuers and it gave phosphorescent lights to the inhabitants of the deep so that they could light their way and attract either prey or potential mates. It provided the bat with the supersonic signals which enable it to fly in total darkness and gave a form of gyroscope to migratory birds so that they could make their prodigious journeys in which their life is spent.

The Elementals of a higher level added beauty to practicality, and bordered the edges of the cloak of the sea with foaming ermine, modelled cities and towers from the clouds and austere faces out of stones. They used every means at their disposal to make the sun dazzle with its brightness by day and the stars, both existing and no longer existing, give beauty to the blackness of our nights. They did not create all of this, since that was beyond their capabilities, but they made it possible for us to admire it and gave Nature the touches of colour and sound which would make our stay in this dimension bearable and even happy. Music, colour, architecture, dance... all these things were harmoniously brought into play by those portentous artists.

The Guardian Angels, another variety of Elementals, placed hope and enthusiasm in our afflicted Souls and, with the help of the Sylphs of the winds, raised the pennants that smell of the bronze of glory and allied themselves with the Gnomes so that we could search for hidden treasures and so that no one should feel irretrievably poor.

They are the ones who, once servants of Anubis or of Charon, today help the Souls at the always difficult times of disembodiment and rebirth into a new life, calling upon the Fairy Godmothers to bestow their gifts on the chosen ones at that moment when the relationship of the heavenly bodies draws arrowheads on the natal charts of the horoscopes.

Up to the age of seven, he is provided with an Elemental who suggests to him, in the manner of an inner voice, what things he should avoid as being dangerous.

# THE GUARDIAN ANGEL

One of the many myths (psychological realities) which Christianity has taken from the old mystery religions and re-used is that which refers to the Guardian Angel.

When a child is born, so the Ancient Teachings say, his higher principles do not incarnate suddenly, but in a gradual manner, with the result that the new arrival does not have an actual mental body and can only use a mental sub-body of his emotional body. This makes him vulnerable in relation to the circumstances of life. So, up to the age of seven, he is provided with the untiring company of an Elemental who suggests to him, in the manner of an inner voice, what things he should avoid as being dangerous. It is a form of manifestation of an intelligent or at least trained instinct, for as we shall be seeing later on, the Elementals are not exactly "intelligent".

It has been represented as a human figure, generally that of a very beautiful young woman with large wings, which in the old symbolism signify "protection" and also "presence of death". Sometimes she holds in her hand a branch of shining nards or simply a lantern.

Discounting the exceptions, only children can see it or perceive it in some way. Its body is extremely plastic and takes on the forms which are most attractive to the child, and if the latter is receptive they teach him games and present him to the dancing Gnomes and the restless Elves who inhabit the corollas of flowers.

The Guardian Angel is another of the many Services which Nature offers to all humans without exception. Unfortunately, over the last two centuries, environmental pollution and the routine way of educating children in the big cities, introducing them into adult life before their time, have diminished Nature's powers of protection and the Guardian Angel has become a rigid and impotent witness to the degeneration of our race.

# THE STRANGE POWER OF KNOTS

In all the ancient representations of magical symbols we shall find interlaced designs, from the criss-cross patterns stamped on the pottery of the Japanese neolithic, to the swastikas of the Hindu temples and the Greek vases, the quincunces of Teotihuacan or the medieval nodes which were later to adorn the hats of Catholic bishops. The sailors of all times have developed an art and a ritual of tying and untying knots, and by the way each one does it, it can be recognised whether or not he belongs to the age-old fraternity of the Sons of Poseidon.

Celtic and Roman amulets show us the fingers of a hand crossing over one another and still today many people do this to ward off evil processes which they sense that fate may hold in store for them.

Some Elementals of the Gnome and Fairy types can be seen more easily through the hollow knot in the wood of an old tree.

The knot and the skein are very closely linked with the world of the Elementals, the Genii and even the great Angels. It is a skein which is woven and unwoven by the Parcae, until the fate known as Atropos cuts the fibre with magical scissors and the marked man dies. It was a knot which the Elementals of History placed before Alexander as a prior condition of his conquest of Asia, a knot which according to some belonged to an enchanted quadriga, and according to others was the remains of a great book of the old nodic culture from far-off China.

It is also a knot which is traditionally tied at the umbilical cord when a child is born, and that is why the "Omphalos" of Delphi appears covered with knots and intertwining cords. The intersection of paths which the Gods offer to Oedipus and where he chooses his tragedy is a knot; a knot also is the crossroads in the Tarots of Egyptian origin, and another knot is the forking of paths which in Medieval mythology appears before the Knight who is in the process of being Initiated.

Thus, throughout the History of Mankind, the knot has always been one of the symbols of its union with the Elementals and with the Gods which rule them. The First Things are not nailed or welded together, but are elastically bound, and when they become functional they make music and exist in the Darkness... They are tied.

## ARE THE ELEMENTALS EXTRATERRESTRIALS?

In spite of all the psychological "opening-up" towards the Cosmos which the 20th century has witnessed, and the physical fact that to date two men have walked on the Moon, and that specialised instruments are probing the solar photosphere and the most distant planets, an arbitrary division continues to be made between the "terrestrial" and the "extraterrestrial". If we were really to broaden our conception of the Universe and see our planet as one more tree in an immense forest, we would be able to understand many things which for the moment are veiled from us.

But the geocentric and anthropocentric outlooks have been with us for a very long time and still carry with them a great weight of inertia. At the time of writing, there are still millions of people who believe that God, the Absolute God, incarnated only once and just among one particular tribe of men on this planet, and at no other place or time. This reduces the "extraterrestrial" to the role of a mere background or container less valid than the Earth.

On the other hand, the growing problems of our century - to which no solution is seen - have engendered a psychosis of "escape forwards", and on the basis of certain observations of flying objects as yet undetermined and unconfirmed, a neo-mythology has been built up about invaders from other worlds which like innocent and at the same time avenging and redeeming angels, would be watching over the evolution of Mankind.

Thus there are some who wonder if the Elementals are of extraterrestrial origin, or if there are Elementals beyond the Earth.

If we look more deeply at the subject of origins, we shall come to the conclusion that we are all extraterrestrials, since it is impossible that the Earth has existed for ever. If the Human Spirit is immortal, it must have lived somewhere else before the Earth existed, and will continue to manifest in other places when this planet has completed its physical cycle and has been destroyed. This does not mean that we arrived in space ships or in rockets like those built by the man of today. The Old Teachings tell us of cosmic migrations of large groups of Souls who move "house", leaving the old ruined one behind and moving on to one that has been newly built and is ready to be used for the obtaining of new experiences.

As the Elementals are a life-form which is different from the human, but a life-form all the same, we must suppose that they too move from planet to planet, from star to star, following the mysterious route which marks out the direction of everything that exists.

We are also told, as we have mentioned elsewhere, that there are Elementals which govern and watch over the heavenly bodies themselves and that we should not confuse these with the Spirits of those planets and stars whose bodies are their more or less spherical forms. The Tibetans gave the name of Chohans of light or Dhyan Chohans to these immense and extremely powerful Elementals which look after the material bodies of the Cosmos. Thus, our Earth has its Dhyan Chohan to govern it, and all the other Celestial Bodies will have theirs. Apart from this, a veritable "fauna" of Elementals live in the extraterrestrial space which official science now recognises, not as an absolute void as was rigorously affirmed until less than a century ago, but as a space which is filled with a kind of atmosphere far more subtle than the air that we breathe; which on the other hand is logical, since the condensation of Matter must be a gradual process, with the result that the distance between particles will be greater in the places furthest away from the centres of gravitational concentration which are constituted by the physical heavenly bodies.

These "computers", far more perfect than any that we know or will ever know, which are the Elementals, are responsible for the automatic maintenance of the whole Cosmos and its inhabitants. They have been programmed by the Gods, who in turn are Children of the enigma which we call God.

We recommend the reader not to believe for this reason that the Elementals are mere machines. Let us remember that our own physical body, as well as the vital, the emotional and the lower part of the mental body, are also kinds of "bio-robots" or "computers" and yet we do not for that regard them with contempt, but quite the reverse... and even to excess.

# CHAPTER VIII

## THE SPIRITS OF NATURE AND OTHER SPIRITS

The term and denomination of "spirit" is as vague and as indefinable as the spirits themselves. It is not matter, it is not energy... is something beyond. It is not only metaphysical, it is also metaenergetic and even pararational. But it is not the aim of this little book to deal with such deep matters; suffice it to say that, when we mention "spirits", we are using the term merely to identify a Being as distinct from a Thing, or at least the less evident forms of Being which we call "Things".

On this humble note, we shall now refer to the evolutionary line or line of life in which the Elementals are to be found.

# DOES EVOLUTION REALLY EXIST?

When, in the 19th century, the evolutionary theory was launched - soon to become a dogma of faith in spite of the warnings issued by Darwin, one of its greatest proponents - it was thought that the golden key to the Universe had been found.

Undoubtedly, the new theory (which had in fact already been known in many of its aspects in the East, from India to Tibet and Egypt, as the West had also known of it in the form popularized by the Pythagoreans) was a most interesting development which swept away many "taboos" that had arisen from the one-track study of the "dead letter" of the Bible. In this work, in a period of six millenniums, the so-called "Old Testament" situates the creation of all known living beings, which go into and out of the Ark and pass down to our days without transformation or adaptation, including Adamic Man; for the man who might have been the product of Cain and the women of the "Land of Enoch", except for a belated connection with the American aborigenes, was not mentioned. The first excavations and detailed studies of the paleontological collections which were already in existence, clearly showed that the planet had been inhabited in earlier times by a different fauna and flora from those which exist today. But the evolutionist wave was so sweeping that it had little time for details and took for granted that Man was not what Darwin had proposed, like an elder brother of the ape, but his actual descendant. The "positivists" socialised the new belief and, with complete confidence, divided the human past into 4 periods, like watertight compartments which excluded one another if they happened to coincide: the first, magical, the second, religious, the third, philosophical-metaphysical and the fourth, the crown, the scientific-positive.

All this, emphatically taught in all the prestigious Seats of Learning and supported by an evident triumph of the Western Civilization over many diseases which had been regarded as "curses from God"; in a world in which everything seemed to be moving violently towards growth and perfection, aided by the heavy-handed opposition of the Churches which gave in when it was already too late and then, with especial casuistry, joined in with the majority of the evolutionary ideas - including political ones - all this brought us into the remarkable 20th century with the absolute certainty that evolution is an unshakeable fact.

But soon the warning notes which had already been sounded in the last century from numerous and different positions began to be heard and analysed. The science of systematic excavation, which we normally call Archaeology, together with the science of museum work, showed that evolution, if it exists, is not something as simple and clearly graded as had been thought, but that it contains enigmatic cycles, apparent advances and retrogressions, the coexistence of forms of magical civilization with those of a scientific and even the most advanced technical kind, a fact which cannot be denied when we are confronted by the evidence of examples as remote as the Pyramids of Egypt and the walls of Sacsahuaman in Peru. As for Man himself, the "missing link" which would connect him with the ape was never found, since the appearance of the measurements with Carbon 14 demonstrated that the famous "Piltdown skull" had been a "puzzle" made as a hoax by students using fragments of the skulls of a negro and an ape and some artificially aged arrowheads. Today we know that, before our own, there have been other very brilliant civilizations and that the much slandered Atlantis, whose last remains are mentioned by Plato, did indeed exist and is submerged in the middle of the Atlantic, although at the time at which I am writing no finds have yet been made - or have not been properly analysed - to demonstrate that it was inhabited by human beings.

In any case, it is evident that evolution exists, although it is contained within the great dance of movements and countermovements which move laterally and independently in search of perfection. It is not the one proclaimed by the "evolutionists" of the 19th century, but it exists and apparently has existed since the very first manifestations... of form. And this is what we want to emphasise. Bacteria, for example,

The Indian esoterists call them "devas" because of their brightness, but also "amanasas" because they are mind-less.

are very simple and unevolved and nevertheless they have remained equally strong for millions of years, without apparent changes. Some fossil insects, specifically the dragonflies of the Mesozoic, are found today encased in their tombs of stone, differing from the present forms only in size. Is it really the form which evolves? Can we not think rather in terms of an increasing awareness of Souls and a greater development of life which makes forms change, just as the successive photographs of a film strip pass rapidly before our eyes, giving us the idea of a continuous and apparently unending evolution? If all things are animate, since the Soul is the reason for the existence of the animate, why have insects not changed their forms like the mammals? Why have bacteria from the Palaeozoic been found which are more or less identical to those of the present?

If plants, animals and men are all Spirits passing through countless reincarnations in search of their own perfection, why do some change so much that we say that they evolve with time and others do not? And even if we deny the Spirit and its reincarnations, in the purest materialistic style of the 19th Century, this will not solve the problem for us since the fossils and their impressions with their contradictory evidence continue to make a mockery of any evolutionist theory... And of any anti-evolutionist theory.

We are left with one possibility of understanding in the light of the Traditional Teaching. It is the possibility that not all living beings are in the same "line of development", or, if we are referring to something more than the mere form, that we are not all in the same "line of evolution".

# THE DEVIC OR ELEMENTAL LINE OF EVOLUTION

According to the Ancient Teachings there are, coexisting on the Earth, no less than 7 lines of evolution. And even among the manifested and visible beings there are differences of evolutionary paths, and the passage of time-experience takes one form in some and another (or no visible form at all) in others.

The Elementals would belong to a Line of Evolution, if we can call it that, which is different from that of Humans. We do not mean that it is "eternally different", but that in the period of time which we can conceive they are different.

One of the principal characteristics of the Elemental Line is that its individuals are not, strictly speaking, individuals, since they lack a Self like the one that humans have; they do not have a mind like we do and therefore they are unable to recognise themselves or to know things in the same way. The Indian esoterists call them "devas" because of their brightness, but also "amanasas" because they are mind-less. They do not have what we call "the voice of conscience", and they do not distinguish morally between good and evil. If they do no harm it is not for any ethical reasons, but because their "programs" do not allow for acts of aggression which would be useless and dangerous for their own perpetrators. But when an aggression is committed against them and the aggression goes beyond the safety limit which is, as it were, impressed on their innermost structure, the Elemental can fight back and continue to do so until the formal extinction of its enemy.

This characteristic of being mind-less makes them, as we wrote before, unafraid of death. But it also means that they cannot savour the honeyed delights of immortality or experience the stinging pains of doubt.

# THE INHABITANTS OF STATUES

The reader will have been struck by the great importance which all the ancient civilizations gave to statues, not only for aesthetic reasons but also because of the magical powers and miracles which they attributed to them. This has not been lost and we can still see, in both East and West, numerous votive offerings made in memory of miracles of healing performed by statues of gods or by images of saints.

When the reformist tendency which appeared with Pope John XXIII, in this 20th century (we clarify this because there was another John XXIII, whom we had better not mention), approached some churches with the proposal of exchanging their battered old images and statuettes for others that would be whole and otherwise exactly like them, the people reacted with their healthy instinct and categorically opposed such changes. In some obscure way the people knew that the old images were "charged" and that the new ones would not be. But... charged with what? What is it that gives certain generally ancient images the power to grant some of the things which they are asked for and even to perform certain miracles which modern science cannot explain, like those, recently studied, of the Virgin of Guadalupe, in Mexico? We know that many hoaxes have been perpetrated, that tiny holes in the faces were filled with wax so that the heat of the lighted candles would in time produce the semblance of tears, and many other things besides. But even the whole range of ancient and modern deceptions does not cover all the "paranormal" phenomena, great and small, that have been registered. Writers from Herodotus to the present journalist-historians still continue to astound us with tales of almost incredible phenomena.

Here also, following the keynote of this short book, we shall have recourse to the Ancient Wisdom, which teaches us that men - or at least some of them - have, since time immemorial, preserved the Magical Art of breathing Elemental Spirits, generally very powerful ones, into statues, which a Magician or a great Artist (who is a kind

*Ancient Wisdom, which teaches us that men havepreserved the Magical Art of breathing Elemental Spirits into statues, which a Magician or a great Artist has encased in marble or bronze.*

of Magician) has encased in marble or bronze and has programmed to assist those who implore the image. To do this they make use of "thought forms", which should not be confused with the Elementals since they are creations of the human mind, but which are used to guide and direct the Elemental involved in the process.

The Spirits of the Statues are not always beneficent. In some cases, either through the intentional will of those who charged the statue or simply by being improperly handled, a rebellion takes place in the objects (was that what affected Lord Carnarvon when the tomb of Tutankhamen was dicovered?) which activates psychological forces unknown to our century, and showers misfortune on the humans and those they love.

Those of us who frequent museum laboratories know from personal experience that the ancient images, amulets and statuettes, are not totally lifeless. They have a kind of life of their own which it is advisable not to contradict. We also know that there have been a lot of tall stories and pure inventions about this subject, which give the idea that a museum gallery is like a room full of bewitched jack-in-the boxes. This is not the case; by night or by day, those who respectfully approach the old statues and amulets and treat them without fear and with the intention of preserving them, have nothing to fear. There are even some ancient exhibits which express their satisfaction with surges of the scent of roses or incense which have no apparent physical source.

The ancients used strange alloys and rare stones, as well as ceramics fired to determined degrees close to incineration (the Sumerian and Babylonian potters were highly expert in the latter process) in order to fix a powerful Elemental in their statues as firmly as possible. Such is the case of the "impossible" alloys used by the Egyptians (called "electrum" by the Greeks) and by ancient American civilizations, like the Mochica and the Chimu, which the Incas called "tumbaga". Objects made in this way can keep the Elemental in a state of potential activity for many thousands of years.

*The "thought forms" of people are able to charge flags and banners, heraldic devices and logotypes which acquire a kind of life of their own.*

The "thought forms" of people, too, simply by their enthusiasm and sacrifice, are able to charge flags and banners, heraldic devices and logotypes which acquire a kind of life of their own, receive and absorb a psychological charge, but also give it out generously when it is necessary. But the thought form is not enough because it would be too ephemeral. It attracts an Elemental and between the two they form an efficient "machine" which acts on the conscious or subconscious of the people. Even what the modern psychologists call the "collective unconscious", is deeply affected by the charged images or even by mere replicas of them.

This would explain the reason why, in spite of having lost their respective wars and not enjoying universal conscious approval, a thousand Hitlerite swastikas are sold for every English or American flag, and a thousand busts of Napoleon, particularly from the time of Waterloo, for every one of Wellington.

The inhabitants of statues, the charges of flags and banners, can be transferred to others, but this is a subject which is too long and perilous to be dealt with in a book which, like this one, is intended for public distribution. Suffice what has been said.

## CHAPTER IX

# ELEMENTALS AND SPIRITUALISM

When Plato was asked if the spirits which appear at crossroads to travellers are superior and beneficent, he replied that they were not, since no human Soul which had left its body and had an elevated nature would be wandering about in the region of this world in search of the earthly sensations which, after death, it ought to have overcome. It is evident that the famous Initiate was not referring to the Spirits of Nature. But can the disembodied Souls of men become corporeal on certain occasions and compete, as apparitions, with the Elementals?

We shall try to answer this question.

We have spoken of the planes of vibration in our Universe. On each of these, Man has a possibility of consciousness which in the case of the four lower planes has already been realised and taken the form of actual bodies, with their sub-bodies which would perform the functions of tissues, systems and organs in different dimensions, within a whole of great complexity and perfection. When the Soul is

These "psychic corpses" usually "descend" on mediums in spiritualist sessions.

withdrawn from that whole, beginning with the lowest of the bodies, the physical, and we say that a man dies, the said bodies tend to dissolve and return to amorphous matter, since they no longer have what we could call the "magnetic" structures which have held them under different forms, maintained the relations between them and regulated them. The biological robot becomes a kind of "scrap" which breaks up into its various components and these, simple and renewed, will then be used to form other living structures in the future, following the law of Nature discovered by Lavoisier whereby "nothing is lost, everything is transformed". This recycling phenomenon is evident in the physical body, since anyone can see how it rots away and how the chemical elements which were formerly held in balance tend to escape, each according to its own nature, with the inevitable destruction of a body which is no longer useful to the Soul, with the result that it loses the vital factor which was reflected in a thermodynamic ecosystem.

The same happens, at the death of man, with his higher psychological bodies, although the phenomenon is not so easy to observe since it takes place on subtle planes to which the great majority of mortals do not have access. But it occurs when the laws of Nature determine it, whether the phenomenon can be observed by many, by few or by none. A piece of iron in contact with water will inexorably rust even if we hide it in a chest and bury it deep in the ground.

Just as the remains of a ruined house may occasionally serve as a refuge for the animals of the countryside, these disintegrating bodies do not always follow the normal course of complete destruction. On certain occasions, this "shell", which the eminent esoterist H.P. Blavatsky calls an "Elementary", can remain almost completely intact, either due to the circumstances surrounding it or else due to some internal variation in the process of decomposition, as happens with the more or less famous uncorrupted corpses.

These "psychic corpses" remain practically whole for a time, with similar characteristics to the ones they had when they were indeed vehicles for a human Soul. And they retain appearances and

*The ancient Pythonesses performed under the protection of hosts of Elementals or Guardian Angels, in special places on the Earth.*

characteristics, memories and aspects of the Soul which inhabited them. These are the ones which usually "descend" on mediums in spiritualist sessions. Anyone who has ever attended these meetings of generally good-natured and religious people (who are only trying to contact their departed loved ones through one or several especially sensitive persons, whose powers are increased by a suitable atmosphere, appropriate music and words and the magnetism produced by the linking of hands of the participants or by their laying them in the same way on a table, or on the arms of an armchair) will have noticed that the words written or pronounced by the medium tend to be faltering and quite often full of "interferences" and interruptions.

There are two further possibilities.

The first, which is the least common, is that the human Soul, either because it has only recently disembodied and is therefore still excessively attached to those whom it has left behind in this world, or because its lack of spiritual development holds it down on the psychic planes for a long time, re-uses the remains of its lower vehicles together with the magnetic-psychic charge given off by the participants in order to manifest itself through the medium. We wish to stress that these practices are of no benefit to the disembodied Soul since they pull it back from its ascending movement and prevent it from attaining its well earned "rest" on the higher plane, "Heaven" or "Devachan", which corresponds to it on the basis of its particular nature and accumulated karmic achievements.

The second case, which is more common, is that, attracted by the spiritualist circle, the Elementary or "shell" is inhabited by an Elemental, a more or less mocking kind of Genie which reflects back the images which are projected onto it, in the manner of a mirror. Such is the case when Elementals come into contact with humans through practices of spiritualism or witchcraft and, either alone or with the help of some fellow tricksters, frighten the people with noises, lights and even with extraordinary movements of heavy furniture. In some cases exceptional phenomena can take place which get out of control for the credulous assembly who provoked them. In those cases, the most practical course of action is to turn on as many lights as possible, open doors and windows to allow air to circulate, and for each one to make his separate way home having learnt his lesson and decided to stop playing at sorcerers' apprentices, since one cannot rule out the possibilities of dangerous accidents and psychic disturbances, above all in the person acting as the medium, which are often irreversible as a result of real damage to the nervous system.

One might ask, however, whether it is ever possible, in certain cases, for the spirits of departed humans to make contact with their loved ones who are still in this dimension, without the need for the dangerous practices of spiritualism.

The answer is affirmative. Yes, they can do so, but it is highly exceptional for them to "come down" to those in incarnation and more likely that by means of prayer and meditation, it will be the Souls of the living who can rise above their lower necessities and achieve telepathic contact with the departed. These were the practices that were performed in the temples of the old Mystery Religions and which, in a much more restricted way, are still achieved by some people in the present, whether through having been taught or due to an intuitive ability in occult matters.

The ancient Pythonesses performed this phenomenon, but under the protection of hosts of Elementals or Guardian Angels, in special places on the Earth and under the direction of a priest who had been initiated in the Mysteries. But the pendulum of the clock of History has done away with all that and the hour has not yet struck for its return, although the time is ever closer at hand and the interest of millions of people in these esoteric subjects portends its coming.

# EPILOGUE

Like all things that are manifested, this Manual or short book has ended. The Author hesitated on several occasions about whether to expound some subjects much more fully or whether to remain totally silent about them so that the reader would pass them by altogether. In the end, with some exceptions, a happy medium was sought which would enable those with the patience to read and reflect on what they had read to gain an unusual insight into what is at present known about the Spirits of Nature or Elementals. And we are not referring to their descriptions in folklore, of which there are some excellent ones, but to what the Elementals really are, regardless of the customs and viewpoints particular to different peoples. Blind fears and beliefs generally give a distorted picture of reality.

As an Acropolitan Philosopher, the writer has tried not to present this as an isolated subject, but as part of a lost cosmovision which was far more natural and decontaminated than the one which is in vogue nowadays. Just as for the archaeologist it is difficult to imagine the correct shape of a vase when he only has a very small fragment of it in his hands, those interested in esoteric subjects will not obtain a solid understanding if they base themselves only on some particular aspect which they find momentarily interesting.

However much we may hate to hear it said, in order to understand Life in any of its manifestations,whether physical or metaphysical, we have to commit ourselves, to revise and clean up our whole scale of values very carefully, and to have the strength to assert solidly what we believe to be valid, and to attack what our judgement tells us is invalid.

Half-tones and half-hearted attitudes are not the happy medium, nor do they stand for equanimity, justice, or goodness... and least of all truth. Extremist tendencies are bad and so are mediocrities. The truth is to be found elsewhere. In a marvellous place which is reached through unselfish effort, through a naturalism without fanaticism, a mysticism without sects and a tenacious and patient spirituality.

It is necessary to study and work hard.

It is necessary to bring back bravery and courage into our lives so that we can really dare to lift the heavy lids which guard the secrets. But remember the initiatic myth of Pandora's Box: he who is not prepared and sufficiently purified, who is impelled only by curiosity or the desire for powers, let him not dare and let him not know, for later he will be unable to be silent.

What the present Humanity is most in need of is a little healthy spirituality, a little peace in the Soul, giving less importance to the body and its passions. But today there are many who speak of maize and corn and forget about frankincense and myrrh. We must help them to recover the balance which has been lost so that our progress towards the future will cease to be darkened by black clouds of evil omen.

"THERE IS NOTHING HIGHER THAN THE TRUTH"